JOY BERKE

TRIUMPH *over* TRAGEDY

COULD THE PERSON YOU LOVE BE A NARCISSIST?

ISBN: 1453889159
ISBN-13: 9781453889152

PROLOGUE

I decided to write this book for a few reasons. It began as a personal catharsis. My later-in-life, almost 10 year relationship had recently ended and I was in despair. I had never felt that much pain before and I had to find a way to grieve, understand and recover. At the same time, as a psychotherapist, I was encountering the same issues in clients and remembered clients I worked with in the past dealing with these same types of people. Most of them were involved in romantic relationships and/or marriages but some were parents or children of narcissists, also struggling to understand exactly what kind of person they were dealing with.

What we all had in common was that the people we were trying so hard to have love us were all narcissists.

Since I write a monthly column for our local newspaper, about three years ago I wrote about Narcissistic Personality Disorder (NPD). I was fully aware at that time that I was married to a man who fit right into that profile. I still held a deep hope that he could change and we could live happily ever after. In my fantasy he would read my article and say "oh my that's me and I'll stop being who I am and become what she needs". How naïve of me. I will be telling you more about my personal story as the book unfolds but that is just a small portion of this book.

Another reason for writing was since I realized I had now become a specialist in NPD, I wanted to share both my knowledge and experience with those who were experiencing similar issues especially in romantic relationships.

Dealing with a narcissist is traumatic for people who want to have intimate, trusting relationships. It is often even more traumatic when the relationship ends. My hope is that this book offers not only compassion and explanation but practical help as well.

It's not written in a 'once I felt that way and now I feel this way' format. The reader will be part of my own growth and my own changing perspective.

Sometimes it was like taking two steps forward and a step back but always moving toward healing and understanding.

Although the chapters were not written in the order in which they are presented the reader will probably be able to track my personal progress, sense my hurt and anger, then my resolve and finally my understanding, acceptance and recovery, making an interesting full circle back to love.

Chapter one is a brief overview of the narcissistic personality. The descriptions are generalizations and you will notice that not all narcissists have all the characteristics to the same degree. Some may have more of them and some, less.

After reading it, you should know whether you are or have been involved with a narcissist. If you find that is the case, please keep reading and hopefully your relationship and your feelings will be explained and sorted out. Maybe your decisions will also become clearer and you will know what the best way to handle your own particular situation is. No two relationships are the same and not every choice will be right for everyone.

The Narcissistic Characteristics (an overview)

One day while in the grocery store ice cream aisle buying dessert for a luncheon I was hosting, I noticed how many different kinds of ice cream there were. I knew one of my lunch guests was on a low carb diet, another was on a low fat diet and yet another was allergic to a certain sweetener. I, at the time, was a vegan and didn't eat any dairy. All the variations were called ice cream but they were all different.

Since I was thinking about narcissism at the time, my realization was that narcissists are like ice cream. They come in many flavors and while some have more or less sugar and others have more or less fat, the basic ingredients are similar and over-all we call it ice cream.

There are two main types of narcissism; the intel-lectual or cerebral and the somatic. They are very different and I will explain each of these in a future chapter.

The Overview

Any given narcissist will have some characteristics and behaviors that are different than any other, but some of these will be consistent and belong to all of them. Two of the characteristics that run through all narcissists to differing degrees is lying and decep-tion. Some lie like most of us breathe. Some lie just because they can.

Some like keeping people confused and off-balance. Some like it when you don't know what reality is and just when you think you know something, they will contradict what they've told you and wonder how you could have thought that they actually said what you just heard them say. Often they will say that even if you did hear them say it, it wasn't what they really meant. You will know you understood the words and ask what else they could have meant. You will not get a satisfactory answer.

Another similarity shared by people with the somatic type of Narcissistic Personality Disorder (NPD) is their charm, which I will discuss in more detail later.

Most narcissists love to have secrets and their need for privacy is boundless. They don't want to be truly known and are most likely afraid that if you know too much about them, you will eventually figure them out and that the secret they most need to protect will be out of the bag. That secret is about how they really see and feel about themselves, and for the most part, they are also keeping this a secret from themselves. So they like building a mystery around themselves and then feel protected by their vagueness and ambiguity.

Another characteristic is their lack of true feelings of compassion. They only have some learned behavior that they've picked up along the way of life that they rely on to get them by when they think they will benefit by showing certain reactions. In truth they really don't know or don't much care what you are feeling. The entire gamut has learned how to act understanding to whatever degree is necessary to serve themselves. Often what looks like acts of kindness on their part are necessary proof to themselves of what 'good' people they really are.

In a relationship with a narcissist, it is common that once you have exhausted your narcissistic supply for them, they will dismiss you and replace you while assigning you a new position in order to assure themselves that you still 'love them' and are willing to serve them in a different capacity. If they still receive any form of ego stroking from you they will want to continue having you in their lives to supply it to them.

As their partner, despite how much they may have professed to love and adore you, you will not feel loved once the initial high is over and you will never feel secure. While telling you of their love and devotion, they will also be telling you what is wrong with you and what you are not giving them. They will insult you one minute and when they have finished, they will be loving and affectionate and wonder why you aren't. They will lie and cheat and push you away and then wonder why you aren't being 'nice' to them. When you remind them of what they've done they may apologize in a casual manner to restore peace or tell you that it was 'history' and you should just let it go.

The concept of it being in the past and letting go is a good one if it comes from a place of love and understanding. But with the narcissist it usually comes from a place of just not wanting to be responsible for his actions and not wanting to be reminded of them or asked to evaluate or explain them. To the narcissist it will be history even if it happened yesterday.

Their apologies are not heartfelt and sincere and they are not really remorseful in any way other than about what they may lose. They are strictly consequence based and never value based which will also be explained in a future chapter.

Because NPD is on a continuum, no two people have it to the same extent or exhibit all the same symptoms. On the very extreme end are socio-paths who have no conscience at all and probably can't even spell the word empathy. To say that only their needs are important would be a gross under-statement. They not only believe theirs to be the most important, but actually the only ones and often those needs are quite pathological. These are not the people I am writing about for the most part although there may be some similarities.

Throughout this book I will be citing examples of both male and female narcissists. However since 75% of all narcissists are men, I will usually refer to them as 'he'. This is not being sexist, merely statistically correct.

Living with a person who has narcissistic personality disorder or NPD can be crazy- making. It can take the sanest, most well balanced people and throw them into mental and emotional chaos. The people in this book have loved and perhaps lived with narcissistic spouses, lovers, parents, children and friends. Their stories are different and yet remarkably similar.

This book also includes a glimpse into my personal journey of loving and living with a person with NPD and how it has affected me and led me to become an advocate of all those who have experienced emotional pain because of their relationship with narcissists and offer help and guidance in any way I can.

When a people are in love with narcissists, they believe they can sense something much deeper than what is being presented to them. However they are most likely not actually in love with a true person. Mainly because very rarely is there a true person actually available to be seen. The narcissist has no apparent self other than the false one she or he presents to the world and to themselves. Since there was never any introspection and never any character development they have not 'grown a self' in any substantial way. Most really have no reachable substance and relationships remain at a maintenance or surface level. That is where they are the most comfortable and feel the safest. They can't help it. If it ever was a chosen way of being, it is no longer.

However, when thinking about how the narcissist sees himself I am reminded of the old philosophical riddle about whether if a tree falls in the forest and there is no one there to hear it, did it make a sound. If a narcissist does not know he is limited, is he? If she doesn't realize that she is living half a life and is happy, is it still a disorder? Does it matter to them or just to you?

This book, however, is not for the narcissist. He cannot be helped because he doesn't want to be; she cannot be changed because she doesn't want to be; he doesn't care what he is missing as it makes no sense to him and he can't understand why anyone else would want it. She doesn't want a contemplative, introspective life anyway. He or she just wants the narcissistic supply to never end. And it usually never does because it doesn't really matter where it comes from. As long as the person giving it meets certain parameters and contributes to the pleasantness of the narcissist's life, that's all that is necessary.

True feelings and attachments aren't there and not really wanted anyway. Sometimes a narcissist actually finds him or herself loving someone to whatever extent is even possible for them. This is not a safe place for them to be. It is often here that they can behave in the cruelest fashion of all. They are trying to prove to themselves that this person can give them everything they need so they test them over and again. Sooner or later the other person must fail. Of course, all of this is on a continuum. Since, as noted no two people have the disorder to the same degree or each characteristic to the same degree.

It is exhausting to be with a narcissist. No matter how much you may love him, it cannot be enough as long as you still have an intact self and needs of your own. You are constantly coming up against the tenuous self that really defines the narcissist. He wants to be close but doesn't want to be seen. The oscillation between hiding and reaching out for assurance becomes a mainstay of the relationship. You can never give him the idealized love that he so badly needs in order to continue to feel valued and when you stop delivering, it becomes your fault because he cannot own any responsibility. That responsibility would undermine what they are desperately attempting to believe about themselves. As mentioned earlier, they of course want to see themselves as good people and will often do little helpful gestures for people to prove to themselves what fine people they are. In this way they can be liked but still be psychologically invisible.

The person's age is also relevant. Narcissists usually get worse as they get older. When adults mature they often become more introspective and take an objective look at their lives as they age. Perhaps they develop new values and goals that are appropriate to their time of life. Narcissists do not do this. If they should sense that their lives are shallow and meaningless, they quickly put it out of their minds and seek even greater ego supply to prove to themselves that they can still live the same type of life that they did twenty or thirty or forty years ago.

This country is actually not a very good place for the aging narcissist, as I will explain later. Youth is the time to begin to develop character as well as personality and unfortunately manipulative behaviors as well. Somehow the narcissist misses this phase of life and only develops surface personality and learns successful manipulations. They learn behaviors that work in order to bring in their needed supply.

One of the characteristics of these behaviors is charm. Somatic narcissists are often romantic and adorable. They have a youthful twinkle in their eye and a sweet smile on their lips. They know that people respond to these and have learned to use them to their advantage. Understand, however, that just because the narcissist smiles in your direction or winks at you or strokes your cheek to them it is a means to an end and that end is always their own needs. Please don't confuse this with a person with an authentic self who uses these same gestures because they actually mean them. There is nothing inherently manipulative about these gestures, the question is about who is using them and for what purpose.

By the way, as long as you don't actually live with the narcissist, the relationship can go on for years. If you are not sharing a home, you are not invading his privacy. He is free to come and go as he wishes and now with a cell phone he can be anywhere. Her private property, whether it be diaries, letters, pictures or whatever are well out of your sight and protected from perusal.

These people are usually the world's best boyfriends or girlfriends. They are charming, warm and affectionate and no one is more fun to be with. They are usually highly sexual and sensual, bring flowers or little (inexpensive) gifts, give lovely but often manipulative compliments and are just absolutely wonderful to be with. Just don't live with them and definitely don't put any demands on them.

Two fun loving people with NPD might have a great relationship for quite a long time as long as the narcissistic supply for each of them is highly compatible. Then each person believes they are getting what they need without actually giving the other person anything over and above what they themselves want to receive. It's a match made in heaven, as long as it is insubstantial on the part of both partners. Some may call it independence but is it? Is it being 'independent' just because no deep attachment is formed? Neither person is really thinking of what they are giving the other except for how it comes back to them. However, this is difficult to maintain if you are looking to actually know and love a real person and grow within a relationship.

This might sound like I am condemning those who strive to get their personal needs met. I am most definitely not doing that as you will see as you continue reading. There is a great difference between healthy, rational self-interest and pathological narcissism as will be explained in future chapters.

The professional diagnostic manual calls narcissism a personality disorder. It is really a character flaw. I will be writing about the difference between personality and character so you can better understand this distinction.

Personality and Character

To make the distinction between personality and character clearer, personality is what a person shows to the world. It is partly innate and genetic and partly learned. You can see the innate/genetic manifestations within the first six months of a baby's life and sometimes even within the first week. If you have more than one child or grandchild you probably have noticed and understand this phenomenon.

Personality can also be viewed from the perspective of 'locus of control'. When we refer to people as introverts or extroverts what it actually means is that introverts are controlled by internal signals and extroverts by external signals. We usually think of an introvert as someone who is shy or a loner and an extrovert as a person who is very social and doesn't like to be alone. In fact there are plenty of outgoing people who are guided internally and many loners who are that way because they take all their cues from external sources and are over-whelmed by all the input they receive. Narcissists are introverts as they take their cues from their own needs. They use outside sources to provide fulfillment of those needs but they do not look out-side to evaluate how they are doing and adjust their behavior. If they are not getting their internal needs met in their areas of concern their supply runs out and they look to new sources.

There is also a 'happiness' level that many psychol-ogists believe people are born with. These happy people will experience sadness the same way that those who are unhappily oriented can experience momentary highs but sooner or later most people go back to the level at which they are most psycho-logically comfortable, unless they make a deliberate choice to change their 'happiness set-point' which is possible for anyone dedicated to doing so. I will say more about this further into the book.

The way a person orients to life is part of their per-sonality. Whether they are optimists/pessimists or realists effects what they bring to social, familial and professional relationships as well. Although these can also change by deliberate intent, there is an in-born element to the way a person approaches their experiences.

Character on the other hand, is who a person is by choice. It consists of values and ethics as well. It is often chosen purposefully as a mechanism for dealing with life, self and other people. Much of the time character is formed at a fairly young age but not always. Sometimes life experiences during adolescence or young adulthood can form charac-ter as well. For example, all children are narcissistic to some extent but highly functioning people grow out of it as pathology and develop a healthy sense of self or a 'healthy narcissism'. Extreme or patho-logical narcissism is a character flaw, although it is called a personality disorder.

People who lie, often called pathological liars, suffer from a character flaw. These people often lie for no other reason than control. They like to feel as if they've put something over on you, that they know the truth and you have been duped. It gives them a superior feeling. And sometimes lying is just easier than accepting the consequences of one's behav-ior. But it is a character flaw. On the positive side, people who value honesty, integrity, the feelings of others, doing good things in the world, etc. are said to have a fine character.

Once a person chooses values and decides to actually live in accordance with them, they have developed their character. This doesn't usually change over the years unless they are faced with a situation where re-evaluation becomes necessary.

Character and personality do not go hand-in-hand. A person can have a great personality and bring great humor, wit and charisma to the table and still have low character and of course this can work in reverse. With the narcissist we are usually taken in by the personality without knowing his/her true character. At least in the early stages of relationship. Once the character has been revealed it is often too late.

The Two Main Types of Narcissists

There are two types of what is called narcissistic personality disorder. They have different appearances and I believe different causes as well.

The Intellectual or Cerebral Narcissist

For the intellectual narcissist it is important that he be seen as smart, right, authoritative, powerful and necessary. He prides himself primarily on his intellectual superiority and feels most comfortable and safe teaching or leading. His goal is not necessarily to impart wisdom or have others learn from what he knows, but rather to receive accolades and respect to supply him with his own narcissistic needs. Equality is not something he strives for with others nor does he want to be around another from whom he can learn. His is the one true word and he often puts himself in a power position professionally so everyone can look up to, respect and admire him and his accomplishments. He views himself as a leader since he believes no one else can do anything better than he can. Unfortunately his confidence and demeanor lead others to believe him and follow. Status in any form is important. Money is important, big houses and expensive cars and clothes show the world how important and successful he is.

If you are his spouse, you must be in awe of him and grateful to him for your wonderful life and he will never let you forget that you are where you are in this life because of his accomplishments.

If you are his child you will most likely be looked upon as an extension of him and must never embarrass him or make him feel unappreciated. You will probably not feel really loved or seen and you will know at some level that you are not a real person to him but you may realize that your power is in being a very important pawn in his game. He doesn't want to lose you and cannot replace you as he can a spouse or lover. You are of his blood and therefore of him. In order for you to live a healthy life, you must disconnect emotionally from both the power you can wield over him and/or the impotence you might be feeling knowing that you are not real to him in any way that counts. I will be speaking more about this in future chapters.

Often his insults are along the line of those around him being stupid, uneducated and perhaps even crazy.

The intellectual narcissist wishes he or she didn't even have a sex drive because they really think sex is beneath them. They would prefer to see themselves as being above such base instincts and when they do engage in sex it is often cold and mechanical. They don't care if you are satisfied and don't need you to see them as good lovers. For the most part they are using someone else's body as a tool of masturbation. Sometimes following a life crisis the cerebral will engage in quite a bit of sex to distance him or herself from the true feelings bubbling up and as a way of getting some kind of narcissistic supply but usually once the crises passes the normal preferred activities of intellectual pursuit to gain adoration and respect will take over again.

The Somatic Narcissist

There is a somatic narcissist as well as an intellectual one. The somatic narcissist is very outwardly different. He is about his body and his senses. He lives on a feeling level and things either feel good or they don't. He's very simplistic and there is no more to life than the physical. He is often an athlete, he works out, he eats well and takes very good care of himself. He will see a physician if he is ill, see a chiropractor to make sure everything is aligned right and care a great deal about his teeth and hair. He loves using his body and his abilities are very important to him. He is a sensualist in every sense of the word. He is fearful of aging and not being able to do all the things that are meaningful to him and that make him proud of himself.

He is often a womanizer although as a misogynist, he has very little respect for women as people. He often holds women in contempt and most likely fears them. He has been know to refer to women as 'toys'.

Having a woman want him is an accomplishment in that he now believes he is controlling and often even demeaning that which he fears. This assuages his need to appear 'more than' and 'stronger than' he knows he really is. He takes what he can from each woman and it is not uncommon for him to have two or three in his life at one time. Usually one is 'primary' and the others 'peripheral'.

The women he chooses are chosen for qualities that serve his supply. That is it! His choices are often women who he believes will raise his status in the area of 'good looks and bodies'. Sometimes he will want to be with an intelligent, respected woman with the mistaken belief that it will raise his. They don't usually choose these types of women because they fear being rejected and don't really believe themselves worthy of a woman of esteem. However, if the woman makes the first overture and he is secure in his knowledge that she wants to be with him, he might venture into that relationship. However, there is more of a chance that a smart, sophisticated woman will see him for who he is and eventually leave him and having a woman leave him is unacceptable to his ego. Most often when the chosen playmate can no longer serve, a new one is chosen and the former given a new role or cast out of Eden altogether.

Unlike the intellectual narcissist, the somatic's insults will be about your physicality rather than your intellect or mental health. He may resort to telling you that you are stupid and crazy as well if he thinks it would work to demean you, but his insult of choice will be about your body, your looks, and your athletic ability.

Sex is one of the main ways a somatic narcissist gets his supply met. However, the women are basically interchangeable as long as they meet the necessary criteria. Early in a sexual relationship the narcissist is pleasing, loving, complimentary and just about everything necessary to secure that the supply keeps coming. His act borders on superb. But he is usually not really connected to the prey and there is no true intimacy and certainly no commitment. It won't matter to him which of his present lovers you happen to be although you will most likely believe you are the only one. Without winning over a new woman, the supply is not as meaningful and isn't enough to sustain him over the long term.

Most somatic narcissists are very affectionate and loving but remember, it is not TOWARDS you as much as it is aimed at themselves getting their supply met. They are especially prone to public displays of affection because having an audience heightens their experience. In that way there are more people seeing how loved and wanted he must be. If the woman is very attractive and desirable that just adds to his feelings that he is special and all other men are jealous of who he is with.

Most somatic narcissists do not marry. They sense that they are not marriage material and that they can't sustain a 24/7 relationship with someone who is likely to eventually see them for who and what they really are. Most of the time they can't even maintain a live-in mate, but marriage with them, if it happens, is destined to be hell unless the spouse knows full well what the relationship limitations will be and chooses to fully accept them. As a rule, narcissists don't know how to be married. They don't understand that in a true marriage there is a protocol of intimacy and support. They are just not capable of that. They are really not 'bad' people, they are just limited in their ability to have deeply committed relationships.

If you are his child, he will put great importance on your relationship but he will not spend much time with you if it interferes with the things he wants to do and the places he wants to go. You are also not real as people but he can't lose you because he has made you a part of him. Remember you are his blood and to a somatic narcissist his blood is part of his body and his body is all he is. You may be extremely angry at him because you have sensed what he is about and have seen how he related to your mother, but you are drawn in to giving him his narcissistic supply also and even though your relationship with him has wounded you very deeply, you continue to maintain it. This will also be discussed in depth later in the book.

Both types of narcissists are often competitive with their children for the attention of the spouse.

If you are an intellectual narcissist meeting an intellectual narcissist the union will probably not progress. There will be too much competition and neither person will receive enough of their supply. If one of you is a somatic and the other an intellectual, it will never work at all. You will both be frustrated and never get your needs met. The intellectual will never give the somatic enough love and affection because the intellectual is not getting enough respect and admiration. This circle will continue until you both cry 'enough'.

If you are a somatic narcissist meeting another, it can work beautifully for a very long time as long as you continue to feed each other at this level. However, if you are not a narcissist at all and believe you've found the perfect partner, after a while you will become frustrated, disappointed and angry. You will often not be taken seriously, not be told the truth and kept at arm's length of the person's inner self (which you will still think exists in a form that can eventually be manifested).

You will constantly be appealing to his better nature and inner goodness and want him to look at himself and learn about why he does what he does. However, he has no better nature in any way that will manifest itself and his inner goodness is buried so far down that no one will reach it, including him. He doesn't want to look at himself and for sure doesn't want to know why he does what he does. He has the sense that there's not much there but doesn't want to really know it. He would like to believe he has substance and depth and will often convince himself of that, but when it comes to proving it, he can't. But again, remember that he really has no idea what substance means to other people. If he truly believes he has this type of depth it means he doesn't have the same definition you do.

Jim

A client of mine who I will call Jim, came to see me about 15 years ago. He had been married to Susanne for about six years. At that time, I knew intellectually what a narcissist was, but I had yet to have an experience with one except for a couple of girlfriends with some of those traits. I might have thought those friends were selfish or self-involved but I wasn't particularly emotionally involved with them so I didn't pay all that much attention. When Jim came to see me, I listened very carefully to what he was telling me about his wife and their relationship. I remember him being very distressed and agitated but what stands out for me now was his immense frustration. He seemed like a trapped animal especially when he got up from his chair and began to pace my office. While walking around, he told me how much he loved her and how much he couldn't stand to be involved with her anymore. He told me he was getting severe headaches and couldn't concentrate at work, he was jumpy and his colleagues were concerned about him but didn't know what to do. In fact, it was one of his co-workers who suggested he make an appointment with me.

He said that every evening when he came home from work he would have to slow down for the last five miles just to compose himself before walking into the house. He didn't know who would be home; whether it would be a critical, stern, complaining woman or an affectionate, flirty girl. And sometimes she would start off one way and within a few minutes, if he didn't respond appropriately she could change her manner. She held no after effects from whatever their last interaction had been. Each segment of their lives was discrete and on no kind of continuum that Jim could feel comfortable with or even understand.

He told me that if there was an unresolved issue and he wanted to bring it up for discussion she would get angry and wonder why he couldn't just forget it. He insisted that most of those types of issues were because of something she had done to hurt the relationship and she didn't want to deal with her words and/or behavior again. He believed he could never make her understand his point of view and why things were important to him. He often wished he could forget and move on as quickly and easily as she did but he was an engineer and problems were there to be solved.

He seemed to desperately want to change the relationship or ask her for a divorce but the thought of leaving her paralyzed him. He couldn't seem to explain the hold she had on him but certainly realized it was there. He tried to explain that when things were good between them, which was less and less through the years, he only wanted to stay and when they were bad he wanted to tell her why he felt how he did but she never found the time to hear him. Those were the times he thought he had to leave. The oscillations continued for month after month, year after year.

Jim and I worked together for about three months and during that time, episodes would occur that had him emotionally reeling. I asked him if his wife, Susanne, would accompany him to one of his sessions. He told me he had already asked her and she did not see where it would do any good since it was Jim's problem and she was trying her best to be a good wife to him. Our sessions were basically a holding pattern. We didn't seem to be making any progress and I couldn't understand why. Jim seemed to be an intelligent man who wanted to have a good marriage. He described a good marriage as intimate, supportive, open and close but said he believed that was not what Susanne wanted although she said she did. Jim believed that what his wife wanted was his adoration and to be allowed to have her way about everything. Whenever the subject of divorce came up I could see the overwhelming sadness on Jim's face. He said he could not imagine being without her although he realized he would be less anxious and frustrated.

Jim had a major conflict. He could manipulate himself into becoming someone that he wasn't but who would please Susanne or he could leave the marriage. He left therapy instead. About two years later Jim called. Susanne had left him. She found someone else who she said was more 'fun' but wanted Jim to remain in her life as a friend. He was trying to maintain a friendship with her but it was causing him terrible emotional pain. She would be strictly a buddy one day and the next time he saw her, she would be sexy and flirt with him. Instinctively I knew that seeing her was bad for him and we worked out a plan for him to withdraw from the relationship. It actually took him a couple of months to see the wisdom in that idea and another few months to carry it out.

At that time I was not as expert in the field of NPD as I have become. It is so obvious to me now that Susanne was a narcissist and nothing Jim said or did could ever have changed the outcome of that relationship. Jim wanted intimacy and openness. Susanne was incapable of giving that to him. He never specifically called her a liar but he always said that she contradicted herself and he could never get her stories straight.

Unfortunately because I knew so little back then about the disorder, I focused more on Jim and how he could handle his situation and also on ways to raise his self-esteem so he would not be so much at the effect of Susanne.

At this point I realize there are many things I should have done differently. It most likely would not have saved Jim any emotional pain and grief but it might have saved him some time and given him the understanding that it wasn't his fault and there was nothing he could have done to change the situation. Ultimately someone will leave the relationship. It is usually the narcissist but not always. As long as the supply keeps coming the narcissist will stay but it is rare for a person to be able to keep the narcissistic supply coming without getting their own needs met as well. They will most likely stop delivering and 'force' the narcissist to end the relationship.

I met Jim about five years ago in a restaurant. He was with his new wife and seemed happy but asked me if he could have a word with me outside. There, he told me that although he believed he was as happy as he thought he could be and that he and Karyn, had a baby daughter, he suspected that he was permanently damaged. He believed that no amount of therapy would help and that maybe time would continue to distance him from his feelings for Susanne. By this time, I was five years into a relationship with a narcissist myself and although I didn't tell that to Jim, I did advise him to read whatever he could on the subject and forgive himself for loving Susanne. Narcissists can be extremely lovable and extremely addictive.

Narcissists and Blame

Neither type will ever take responsibility for any of their bad behavior. They will most likely blame you for everything that has gone wrong with the relationship and in a strange way they will be able to justify it. Everything they say will ultimately be correct. The only thing they would have left out was how your behavior evolved because that would have put the responsibility squarely on their shoulders. They cannot see how they have driven you to the behaviors you have acted out, but they most likely will be right about those behaviors. And just in case you think you could have controlled your actions and attitude, please believe that they would have escalated theirs until they got the response they needed from you in order to test your unconditional love for them or until you left or until you failed and they left. But again, remember, they do not know this on a highly conscious level.

They need to do what they do if you are getting too close to actually wanting to know them or having the audacity to ask them to explain themselves or the nerve to confront them in a lie or contradiction. They will very cavalierly tell you the reasons they did what they did or said what they said, but upon reflection (yours of course) it will make no sense and will in reality explain nothing. Then, if you want a resolution you will have to ask again and again and again and be told you are harassing them. At some point you may drop it, but you will know you didn't receive a satisfactory answer and so you will probably withdraw some of your narcissistic supply and then be told that you are cold and unaffectionate.

Please understand that you will never get the truth from this person and the only way to keep any semblance of harmony is to not confront them and continue to be kind and loving to them while you go slowly crazy and become suspicious of everything he says or does. This is the outcome that occurs in most cases. It will only be otherwise if, once again, you accept the parameters and are able to live with them without reacting negatively.

Some people, especially those who understand the disorder and remove their own egos from the relationship, opt to stay in it because they have learned what is possible and not possible within that relationship and believe that what is available to them is enough for their own happiness and well being. They don't want to change the person and accept him or her for that which they are. If this is you, just make sure you have no hidden agenda because it will not be fulfilled. Sometimes a person just makes the decision that being with the narcissist offers enough and more than they would have without the person they love. As long as they are honest with themselves and realize that another person is not responsible for their own good feelings I believe they can make it work for themselves. It is definitely not a decision to be taken lightly and is not for everyone.

In order to keep believing in their own 'goodness' they will continue to deny any part in any altercation. They will justify all their actions and find a way to blame you for driving them to do what they did or tell you that they were deceptive in order to save you from bad feelings. They will never answer the question of, why, if they think you would be upset by their actions, they did them anyway. The answer to that question would put them on a path they do not want to walk. It is the path of introspection and they will not go there. If they do, they know they will inevitably feel bad about themselves so they reach for defensiveness in the form of denial and justification. If you find a deception they will even go so far as to tell you that your pain is your own fault because you should have kept your nose out of their business and if you didn't find out you wouldn't be feeling any hurts. This is obviously a true statement and if you want to live that way, it is of course your choice to do so.

If you are getting too close to making your point they will most likely attack or withdraw. This will save them from the path of introspection which would lead to the bad feelings that no narcissist can tolerate.

Of course this behavior will take them away from the person from whom they really want closeness and unconditional love. They don't see how this works since they believe they are somehow enti-tled to receive it regardless of the fact that they are contributing nothing genuine to the relationship. They then must blame you for this lack of closeness and the withdrawal of affection. Because of their NPD they are unable to see this any other way or change their way of being. It becomes much easier to eventually change the person from whom they want their narcissistic supply to be met. At that point they will leave the relationship and move on to another.

They have no perspective regarding how they have brought about any relationship outcomes. They appear to be unable to see the effects of their behavior going from themselves towards another person. The only perspective they have is from the other person towards them.

If they receive what they need they feel good and if they don't, they feel bad. It is impossible for them to see outgoing effects that travel from them to you. If you are a person who can understand that relationships are always two-way and people inter-act on a variety of levels you will find it difficult to understand that to a narcissist it is only about them and what they are or aren't getting.

Therefore if they aren't getting whatever it is that they need, it must be that you are somehow responsible. They just cannot (as in unable to) see the effects of their actions and how they lead to your withdrawal of the narcissistic supply. They will never ask themselves what part they could possibly have played in your change. They might criticize you and your behavior towards them before leaving you but if you don't agree and change they would rather leave than look at themselves. There will always be someone else out there to take over your role.

Also, no matter how many times they have recreated the same scenario they will still not be curious about it. Each event is discrete and has no connection to any other. They seem not to be able to see patterns of behavior and even if something happens repeatedly and with different partners they will honestly tell themselves that it is the fault of the partner and not of themselves.

You will often hear them say that women (or men) are a certain way and that is why they can't maintain a relationship.

The only people they don't blame publicly are their children. Since their children are extensions of them, they cannot be held responsible either. Also, if their children are wrong about something, in some self-referential way (I will write about being self-referential in another chapter) they would also be wrong and that cannot be. So by extension the children are also blameless. They will make the same type of excuses for their behavior as they make for their own. It is a very interesting phenomenon to observe from afar but when you are involved with it personally, it is difficult to deal with.

In private they will make the child as responsible as they make everyone else. If the narcissistic parent is unhappy and not getting his or her supply from the child then it is the child's fault. Once again the narcissist will be blameless. Until and unless the threat of losing the child occurs. Then the narcissist cannot let that happen and will manipulate the child back into the fold. An internal conflict will occur here because the parent will have to back off on the issue of blame toward the child and find a way to keep him or herself blameless as well. Often the parent will verbally accept the blame but never evaluate it in any meaningful way.

I certainly wish I understood more about the narcissistic parent/child relationship when I was married. It would have saved me a great deal of emotional pain and my own behavior would most likely have been different. When you understand that some things cannot be other than they are and nothing you do or say can change them, your choices become much easier to make. I know now, that I was looking at my situation from a standpoint of 'normalcy' and at the time, did not have the clarity to see that the orientation of a narcissist is anything but what most of us would consider 'normal'. I also see now, that I was in turn blaming him for something he could not control or change either.

I believed at that time that my husband was making a choice-one that he knew hurt me over and over-but from where I stand now and from the perspective I now have, I know he wasn't making a choice at all. What looked like deliberate behavior was merely another facet of the disorder. I cannot and do not continue to blame him for that behavior and have put the entire issue to rest in my mind and heart.

The Narcissistic Addiction

Through some of my research I learned that loving a narcissist is on a par with being addicted to drugs. I believe it. Upon meeting the NPD person initially, you will believe that you have finally found the ideal person. How did you get so lucky? At first blush, he is wonderful. He will charm you with whatever he believes will appeal to you. They are very good at figuring out what that is and delivering. There's an old saying in sales about finding out what is really important to someone and setting yourself up as the only giver of whatever that is.

John Bradford, the addiction therapist once said that if you find out a person's greatest weakness and play to it, you can own that person. That's what the narcissist is so good at. Since they are a step removed, they are good observers. They are also the penultimate interviewer. Without telling you anything much about themselves, they will ask all the pertinent questions about you. That will tell them first, if you can be the one to supply their ego with what it needs, and second how to lure you in by giving you what you have just told them you needed.

The drug effect works differently for each relationship but usually because the onset of the relationship was so exhilarating endorphins begin to flow through our brains. This happens in all early love relationships and ebb and flow as the relationship progresses until it reaches a maintenance level of basic positiveness. Because the relationship with the narcissist becomes so turbulent and chaotic our brain chemistry goes haywire. We long for the days of high endorphin activity. We want to bring back the wonderful feeling we had believing we were loved and adored. We want to feel the ecstasy we felt early on. When we are not feeling that way, we are experiencing a sense of withdrawal. Most other relationships go through the withdrawal stage slowly; so slowly that we hardly even know it's happening until years go by and we notice that we are not head over heals any more.

In the relationship with a narcissist, it happens all at once. An event will usually trigger it where we realize we don't even know the person we love so much and that we were deceived and betrayed by someone we believed loved us more than anything in the world. Those endorphins spin out of control all at once. Our world has gone off its axis. We are thrown into withdrawal.

To be somewhat technical here for a moment, researchers were able to show a connection between romantic love rejection and a cocaine craving with the use of brain images. The research team, headed by Dr. Helen Fisher, used MRI to monitor the brain activity of college age individuals who had been rejected by their partners, claimed to still be in love with the former partner and hoped to reunite. These individuals were shown pictures of the former partner and several areas of the brain were shown to be effected.

These areas were the ventral tegmental area which controls motivation and reward, the nucleus accumbens and prefrontal cortex linked to cravings and addiction, especially to cocaine and the insular cortex and anterior cingulated associated with pain and suffering.

Over time the part of the brain linked to attachments became less active when participants saw pictures of the former partner again.

This research was not done for former partners of narcissists. I believe the addiction process is much more severe when having dealt with a person with NPD. I am not a researcher but I wonder how these tests would fare using participants strictly involved with narcissists whether or not the relationship is continuing or has ended.

But we have become addicted to that person so instead of taking that first episode and thinking 'how can I continue being with someone who has lied to me about something so important' and cutting our losses and leaving, we attempt to renew the relationship. We believe what the narcissist tells us and how sorry he is and that it will never happen again and we return to the safety of his arms. We are mainlining again.

We make excuses to ourselves to keep the drug flowing and the cycle begins. It may go on for years at that level. More lies are discovered, more deceptions are uncovered, we go through withdrawals that are so painful we think we won't be able to deal with another one but soon the ups and downs,

bad as they were, turn into utter chaos. The stronger and saner we are, the harder it is to deal with the narcissist's behavior. We cannot understand it on any level that makes sense to our non-narcissistic way of thinking. Often, in times of clarity we know we have to leave but knowing it is the right thing to do and actually doing it are two different things. We can't seem to bring ourselves to cut off the drug completely.

But the inevitable happens. The narcissist has had enough. Remember, the only thing that really matters to them is getting their narcissistic supply and it has run out. Not only are you not providing what they need any more, you are actually doing the worst possible thing and upsetting them. They are not feeling good. Perhaps you are pushing them to see their own part in this and they would much rather continue to blame you. Whatever the reason, they are done.

One thing is for sure with them. Under all but the most unusual circumstances, they never, ever look back. Once they have made the decision to end the relationship they will never look at it again. It is most likely that they have already replaced you with a new source of narcissistic supply because one of the worse things for them is no continued ego-stroking. They will go from one person to the next the way other people change their clothing. Their capacity or ability to really attach and connect to someone is limited. Most relationships with non-narcissists have their normal ups and downs and the people find themselves facing difficult times and differing opinions and perspectives. This is a natural part of relationships. The narcissist doesn't want to deal with these types of issues and work them through with understanding and caring. The narcissist would rather find a new beginning with a new person and start the thrill of the conquest all over again.

They actually say they want to be alone, but that's the last thing they can be for very long. Having no one to supply their ego with its particular need is torture to the narcissist. It is probably true that they don't want to live with anyone full time because then they will have to deal with giving up their privacy again but true aloneness is completely unacceptable to them. They will often make up reasons as to why they 'want' to be with someone but the reasons are only justifications to themselves for things they don't want to own or admit. Often they will point to their 'alone time' as being contradictory to the fact that they must always have someone there for them. They probably do like their solitary time but it is only because they know it is not a permanent condition and can change whenever they wish it to or need it to.

Leaving the Narcissistic Relationship

So the relationship ends and you are left in total addiction withdrawal. What happens next?

Here's the way it usually goes. Narcissists don't, as a rule, leave with total closure. They would rather assign you a new role in their life. Let's be friends is often the next step. Don't do it. I know you think that maybe you can win him back but you can't EVER. And that is a good thing. I know you don't believe that yet, but it is. The main reason they want to be your friend is to exonerate themselves. This way they can think they didn't do anything really ugly because you are still their friend.

The second reason is because you still might serve as a supplier to them in this new capacity. They probably did like something about you that was giving them part of what they needed and now they think they can have that while not dealing with the part of you that was unpleasant to them. Since you will not win them back because they have completely dismissed you from that role why would you want a narcissist as a friend?

Yes, they will be helpful and kind to show you once again how wonderful they are. If you are paying attention it will remind you of when you first met them and they gave you what they knew was important to you so you would love them. Well, that's what they are doing again. Because it is the end of the relationship as you knew it, you will not ever again be in a position to put any kind of emotional demands on them and since you are no longer living with them, you will not know much about the rest of their life so they now feel free and in a position to be 'nice' once again.

They also want you to continue to care about them so they will feel good about themselves. For your own mental and emotional health stay away from them. It is said that the only way to leave a narcissistic relationship is completely and totally. Cold turkey. The withdrawal will be awful. Someone referred to it as a mild to moderate form of post traumatic stress syndrome. I am not surprised. Please take it that seriously and give yourself lots of time and tenderness. If you need medication, take it. I'm not a physician and hate recommending meds but a small dose of Ativan works wonders when fear and anxiety strike. You may also experience physical symptoms like nausea, stomach pain, loss of appetite, sleeplessness, headache, tremors and chest pain. Take it all seriously and be good to yourself. Do whatever you have to do except have any communication with the NPD person. You are severely wounded and need to heal.

Once you are healed completely you can revisit what works for you but make sure you are grounded and have no illusions about changing the narcissist or the relationship.

Of course, the other side of the coin is that most relationships with narcissists do not end until and unless you want them to. It is often difficult to admit the part you have played in the demise of the relationship. But if you think about it you will realize that if you continued to supply them with their ego needs they would have stayed. They may not have stayed faithful, but they would have stayed.

You most likely withdrew your supply and they no longer wanted to stay with you. It will be in your best interest to own that.

I will relate an understanding of this that I had myself in the midst of going through more emotional pain than I had ever experienced before.

About 22 years ago I had taken a course developed by Robert Fritz, where I got to make formal choices about what I wanted in my life. One of the choices, among others, was the choice to be healthy. It was called a fundamental choice and became the orientation for my behavior. Growing out of that were the choices to eat well, exercise, take vitamins and supplements, avoid risky behavior, get appropriate tests on a timely basis and meditate.

My interactions with my husband were undermining my health. I knew this explicitly. I knew my blood pressure was on the rise, I was constantly angry and stressed and was beginning to have stomach pain. But I still couldn't bring myself to leave him although I would say I was going to and even went to see an attorney. I became someone my family, friends and I didn't recognize. I became a rager; I became sarcastic; I became nasty; I felt awful but I still didn't leave. But I knew he would. I knew as surely as I knew my own name, that he could not and would not put up with this behavior of mine forever. I was making a choice by default without actually owning it. Even subconsciously my decision to be healthy played itself out.

It was actually more important to me to be healthy than it was to remain with him regardless of my feelings for him. So I got what I needed but it took quite a while to let it into my consciousness.

I wanted him to stay but I wanted him to stay and be a different person. That was what I was holding on to for so long. I always thought that if I just said the right thing he would understand and see what he was doing to me and our marriage. Even when I knew it was impossible for him to be any different than he was (because he didn't want to be) I still tried. Someone once said that the definition of insane is doing the same behavior over and over and expecting different results. If that is true I was insane. You probably are as well. I continued to believe that because I saw the potential in him and I felt that soul connection that it mattered to him. It didn't. I will repeat that the only thing that really matters to narcissists is getting their needs met. They don't want to grow and meet the potential that you believe is there and they don't want to relate at any kind of deep or intimate level.

When an addict or drug abuser reaches bottom, he or she must find a way to detox and never again touch the drug of choice. There are facilities they can enter and programs they can join. They have sponsors and/or counselors to help them and spiritual guidelines to follow.

Unfortunately, as far as I know, there are no such facilities or programs for the partners or ex-partners of narcissists. There may be support groups but I have not found one.

Your attachment/addiction to your narcissist is no less than these other forms and so I believe the chapter on recovery will be very helpful.

Meghan

Meghan was almost 50 when she came to see me. I was a few years older and had just entered into my own relationship with the love of my life. I hadn't seen him in 40 years but we were together at last. I had no idea at the time what I was getting into, So even knowing about the illness, I was still able to fall prey. But this is Meghan's story.

She said she was on the threshold of leaving a marriage of 25 years. She was bright and educated and quite attractive. She had two daughters and a son who supported the decision to finally leave her narcissistic husband. She said she was at the end of her very long rope but still loved him. She said she finally realized that he wasn't going to change and be the person she believed for so many years he had the potential to be. Why did I not believe her?

She sat in my office the first visit and just cried. She couldn't even tell me her story. In fact it wasn't until the fourth session that she began to talk. The first thing she told me was that she didn't trust anyone. She let herself just sit and cry because she couldn't do it with friends and family but felt comfortable just letting out her sadness with me. It took months until I was able to put together the entire story.

She was sad, she was grieving, but she was also ashamed. Meghan was a woman who prided herself on her intelligence and emotional strength. Now she felt stupid and weak. Looking back over her marriage she admitted she allowed herself to be abused on one hand while becoming an emotional abuser on the other. This did not coincide with the woman sitting in my office but I knew to what lengths living with a person with NPD could drive a normal person.

She told me about their meeting and how handsome and charming he was. She was the envy of all her friends. After a few years she wanted to marry. He said he wasn't ready as he felt too young and was still in school. They married, however, at her insistance and from that time on he changed. He became withdrawn and demanding one minute and loving and kind the next. If she questioned his behavior he got angry and insulted her. The insults led to pushing her around and yelling. She wanted to leave him early in their marriage but he always convinced her to stay with him and because she loved him, she did.

Meghan told me that things improved after their first child was born and remained stable after the second quickly followed. Her husband enjoyed the children but he was doing his own hobbies and other interests more and more. If he didn't have his alone time and his privacy he would return to treating her badly. If she berated him for not spending enough time with her and the children he would once again insult her and rage at her. After their third child was born, he became more and more distant and she became more involved with the children. Arguments ensued on an almost daily basis. She tried to make him understand what her needs were, what she wanted from him, but to no avail. She told me he might have understood the words, but could not seem to connect to what she was saying on any kind of emotional level or just didn't really care. What he knew for sure was what he wanted and was not getting from her. She said she would have willingly given him what he wanted had he just made an attempt to understand her. They reached a stalemate where they remained for a while. Then things started down the slope again. Each time she mentioned what she needed he would first withdraw and go into another room. When that didn't stop her, he insulted her; when that didn't stop her, he would begin to scream and then push her out of the way and oftentimes just leave the house.

They didn't want to divorce because of the family. The effect on the children was probably more negative than a divorce would have been, but I will write about that later. They tried marriage counseling years before and he charmed the counselor while Meghan believed she seemed like the bitchy, dissatisfied wife of a wonderful man. She was told that he needed to have his privacy in order to unwind after a hard day. She asked if 'privacy' extended to the secrets she believed he had. He told the counselor he had no secrets and Meghan thought the counselor believed her to be a paranoid woman with no life outside the house and jealous of her husband's career. So Meghan went back to work as soon as the children started full day school. It helped her as a person but did nothing for the marriage except give them something else to fight about, which was her income.

She began not to trust him. She said she caught him in some lies that he tried to explain away but his answers didn't make sense to her. He stayed out late always making excuses or he stayed in his garage with his hobbies. But if she got interested in something he wanted her to give it up and pay more attention to him. She wouldn't and their lives became more and more separate.

It was difficult for her to talk about the physical abuse. She seemed to do better with describing the emotional and mental abuse she was put through. She said he never 'punched' her or 'slapped' her, as if this made what he did do OK. He would push her up against a wall or onto the floor and scream at her while the children watched. They would try to support her but were afraid as well. They began to hate him as well as love him. When they reached their teenage years, they would also try to reason with him. They were afraid for their mother's safety. He could not understand the fear, hurt and anger he caused in his family. He insisted he did nothing wrong or if he did that he was 'driven to it' by the harassment of his wife and children. The family was only calm when he wasn't around. But Meghan still couldn't leave him. This is the hold the narcissist has over those who love him.

I finally realized that she wasn't in my office to learn how to leave, but rather to learn how to stay. She was still waiting for him to change, to grow up, to develop values that would coincide with hers. She was still waiting for him to really love her at that intimate, deep level that she needed so badly. I thought of Jim and told her his story. I told her what I knew of the narcissist and how they will never change. Her grief was palpable. I wanted so much for it to be different but I knew it would never be.

Her story ends the same way as Jim's. Her narcissistic husband finally left her. She called me when he did and we worked together for another few months. By this time I was getting glimmers of my own life which I will tell you about soon. Interestingly enough she told me the same thing Jim did when we spoke outside the restaurant. She said she believed that no matter what happens in her life, who she meets, or where she goes, she will always carry a broken heart with her.

The Narcissistic Parent

If it is one of your parents who is the narcissist, this chapter is for you. Most likely your parent will be divorced or in a very unhappy marriage that has effected you deeply.

As a therapist and a divorced parent myself, I have never believed in using your children as a pawn against an ex-spouse. Just because you have divorced your spouse, you can't expect your children to. I have readjusted my position when one of those parents is a narcissist. I now believe that as soon as a child is old enough to understand, he or she should be told what NPD is and how it affects those exposed to it.

If the family is intact, it is likely that the parent with NPD is wrecking havoc on everyone especially the spouse and that the children have been exposed to what they see as crazy behavior on the part of both parents. The literature says that NPD people are not 'usually' abusive. First of all 'usually' is the operative word here and second of all, it depends upon your definition of the word. They certainly are abusive emotionally and verbally and can become physically abusive if pushed. If the non-NPD parent is strong and still sane, and still of the mind that something can get through to the narcissist and keeps trying, that will be interpreted as pushing. Any harassment will be looked at as pushing. Any demand for answers that are true and make sense will be looked at as pushing. At that point the narcissist can get abusive. It will also not matter if there are children present. They are out of control at that time. To the narcissist when that behavior is no longer elicited from him it is an indication that the relationship has lost all meaning and is over. To the partner, it can be taken that the narcissist is finally backing off and 'looking inward'. No, that is definitely not happening.

So what are the children seeing and thinking? And is it better if the parents divorce and end the craziness that the children are witnessing? Before I tell you about the now adult children of NPD people,

I want to make another point and that is that children brought up in NPD homes have similar addiction disorders as do the spouses or partners of narcissists.

If you read the literature on adult children of alcoholics or drug abusers you will see certain threads that run through all of these. These children are usually either very repressed emotionally and find it difficult to make deep attachments also or they are emotionally volatile.

They may marry and have their own families but often are needy and/or marry needy people. They have issues with emotional closeness and tend to keep a certain distance. They tend to be very attentive and affectionate parents especially to babies and young children but may have difficulty relating to their offspring when they become teenagers and/or adults. They are often successful in their careers but again keep emotional distance. They may appear to be very 'adult' on the surface but have deep seated emotional issues that they have assigned certain people to take the brunt of. The scapegoat is often symbolic and has nothing to do with the causality of their problems

They usually realize that the NPD parent has difficulty in relating on anything but a superficial level and conversations are often strained and limited to material, mundane topics. The NPD parent makes a better grandparent than parent because small children are not as threatening and have not seen the grandparent in any type of narcissistic role and are emotionally safe to be around.

The children usually have contradictory feelings towards the NPD parent. On one hand they hate the parent for the havoc they caused in the childhood home and direct all blame on that parent. On the other hand, because the narcissist is so charming and loving (if somatic) and powerful (if intellectual) they also have great love and/or respect for that parent.

Sometimes these adult children make appointments with therapists but often they feel embarrassed by the situation in which they found themselves and have learned to ignore the elephant in the living room while pretending they have a Brady Bunch family to the outside world. When their suffering becomes overwhelming and interferes with their lives, therapy is very much in order and should be pursued. It is a good idea for the whole family minus the NPD parent to come to family therapy where they can support and understand each other and the illness.

It is somewhat different when the parents are divorced. I believe the non-NPD parent needs to explain to the children that what the NPD parent has is an illness and they cannot change it no matter what they say or do. They should be told not to take it personally as it is never about them although the hurt they feel will indeed be personal to them.

Then the non-NPD parent must make every attempt to show the child that he or she is loved for who they are regardless of the sickness of the other parent. If the child is young and in custody of the NPD parent this is indeed a thin line to walk. I can appreciate how difficult it must be to insist that the child respect and obey this parent while understanding this very insidious illness. This child will never feel loved by the parent because the parent can only use the child as he or she uses everyone else in his or her life. Once the child knows that the parent lies and deceives they will never again be trusted. Imagine being a child living with a parent that you can't trust or believe. It is hard enough when you are an adult to do that. When you are a child it is a living nightmare.

What makes the situation even worse in a divorce is when the NPD parent is the custodial one and because the healthier parent has such a difficult time relating to and dealing with the former spouse he or she abandons the children as well. I don't think the non-NPD parent believes the children will have a problem living with the narcissist. This parent probably believes the fault was strictly within the marriage and the relationship between the spouses. Unfortunately the severity of the disorder was not realized and the effect on the children not understood. Sometimes a custodial narcissistic parent will move the children far away from the healthy parent in order to have more influence and 'ownership' of the children. This, of course, has a long-term impact on the children and their adult lives.

One very important factor with narcissistic parents is that since they have never matured they are unable to parent appropriately. Their own needs will still prevail and the needs of the child will always be secondary. As in the children of substance abusers, they wind up taking care of the parent thinking if they fulfill the parents' needs they they will be loved and cared for. If even adults don't usually understand that the narcissist is unable to love them the way they deserve to be loved, can you expect a child to? The child will feel invisible and insignificant unless he or she is a supplier of the narcissistic supply. Then their importance will hinge on whether the supply is enough at any given time.

Often the children are assigned different roles to keep the parent happy. If the child seems to be very much like the parent, especially in looks and preferences, they will be seen as extensions of that parent to a greater degree. In this way they will be approved of more and have more time spent with them. However, if they veer from this similarity they will be treated with even more disdain than the other children because their differences will be seen and taken as a rejection of the parent.

For the children who are dissimilar from the narcissistic parent, they will be criticized and told they are disappointing the parent. They will continue to attempt to please the parent by supplying more and more of their ego needs until they will give up in resentment. At that time the narcissistic parent will attempt to reel them back in because whatever supply they were fulfilling is better than none and the parent really cannot bear to not have a relationship with an offspring since they are part of them and their rejection is much more anxiety producing than rejection by a spouse, lover or friend who is easily replaced. Since with other relationships, they find a way to blame the other person, they cannot blame their child and this leads to leaving only themselves to look at and they can't do that either. So they will do anything rather than alienate a child.

Either way, as written earlier, the children realize that they are not appreciated and seen for the people they really are and know they cannot have more than a superficial relationship with the parent.

However, with some children of narcissists, they are themselves, unable to have more than superficial relationships because they have cut off their own appropriate emotional responses.

Often, because they have never been loved and appreciated for who they are, they believe they must always bring something to the table. Whether it is personal or professional they will always be looking for someone to appreciate them but because they are always in the mode of 'supplying' something they don't get the opportunity to really feel loved for themselves. It becomes a vicious cycle because that which they crave they are unable to allow to be satisfied.

Supplying someone they love with what they need has become a way of life for them and they find it difficult to stop because they believe that once they do, their own supply of love will cease.

Often they will become the romantic partner of another narcissist since it is a very familiar interaction and one that they know and understand.

However, as with other types of multi-generational abusers and addicts, often the children of narcissists become narcissists themselves as you will see from the chapter on 'onset'. The circumstances are right for the children to take on the disorder and so it goes around and around through the generations.

I had asked a former client of mine, who I will call Amanda, to add her story to this book. She preferred putting it in her own words so this is what she wrote, along with the note she sent me along with her story.

From Amanda

This was not something I had any motivation or desire to write and it was miserable even getting these two pages out and we both know I can normally write a novel. I hope you can use at least part of it.

My mom is not my best friend. She is the LAST person I would think to go to in a time of need or even if I just needed good advice. If I want to be a good mother or a good partner in the future, I will pretty much do exactly the opposite of what my mother would do. I describe her in no uncertain terms as emotionally stunted and I do not say that to make fun of her or to be malicious. It is just the way it is.

My sister and I are the most aware that we do not have a typical 'mom' It may affect my brother less or he may just not talk about these things with us. My sister always dismisses any conversation about her by saying that she has nothing to compare her to, which is not completely true. We have friends, other family, even Facebook (as other people have moms). Someone they enjoy their time with (at least by their late twenties), seek advice from, even ADMIRE. To put things in perspective, my sister and I are quite annoyed by the idea of our mother believing she has anything to do with out successes. Without some strong genes that make it quite apparent that we did come from our mother, I doubt anyone would be able to convince us that we were not adopted. And to make it very clear that we are not rebellious teenagers, my sister and I are 40 and 30 years old respectively. And we would REALLY like to get along with our mother and have that relationship in our lives, but it is simply not the hand we were dealt.

I speak about my sister so much when discussing my relationship with my mother not only because my sister practically took over as my mother in my late teens, but also because our relationships are so different with my mother (another apparent affect of my mother's narcissistic traits). My sister is actually much more kind and responsive to my mother, always doing what she asks or what she expects and always listening to her. But, I have a 50 foot wall up between me and my mother at this point. I have as little interaction with her as possible. Her opinions or desires do not affect me. The most I do is try not to hurt her purposefully and only because it seems cruel to make your mother cry. I continue to be angry enough that I would want to hurt her, but that is not the person I want to be. I believe in forgiveness but I have not reached that point yet.

Despite my terrible attitude towards her and my sister's efforts for her, she has done truly despicable things to my sister over the years (though these are isolated events, not everyday occurrences) and oddly tries (fails, but tries) to be her version of nurturing to me.

My sister received truly life-changing, devastating news and told my mother over the phone. My mother literally hung up the phone and did not call her back for three weeks. As a narcissist she did not want the comfort of her life disturbed by my sister's situation. That was the first real break in our relationship. I started to realize the limits that my mother has are not a result of my teenage rebellions or my bad attitude but are about her personal limitations. I try my best to understand that she is not capable of more. She did not have the best childhood. She did not have a role model. But I don't believe my mother tries to do what she can for the sake of her children regardless of whether she had an example of what that looks like, and that is why I have yet to reach a place of forgiveness with her.

Not long ago my therapist asked me to look at some literature on narcissism and I discovered that my mother's problem has a name. For years I described her as a pathological liar, a 5 year old and an incredibly selfish person. I called her ridiculous for her extravagant exaggerations. This was before I realized she is not a rational person you can debate with and perhaps change her mind, nor is she someone who can discuss things in order to come up with the reasonable solution.

I

I separate myself as much as possible from my mother now. I got her to stalk me via text rather than call me incessantly. Occasionally I respond, usually with no more than "I'm fine". My mother does not 'know' me. She knows what I do for a living, what schools I graduated from, that I am not married and not overweight. I think those things are all that really matter to her. She does not know what is important to me, my hobbies, what I enjoy or even what foods I like. I used to be her favorite. I am apparently her spitting image. I do NOT see it, but I guess she would like to believe it. But now that I am approaching thirty alone with no prospects for marriage, I think I became her worst nightmare. I'm happy to fill that role since it means she leaves me alone.

Dealing with her is incredibly draining. It's as if you are talking to a child, but one that refuses to actually take any advice or really listen to you at all.... ever. And that mat sound a lot like most children, but most children do not earn salaries and have 401Ks at their disposal to fulfill your worst nightmares. Most children are not approaching retirement. Most children are not supposed to be your mom.

My mother showed up at concerts, recitals, games. She always wanted to throw the big birthday or graduation party. But she has no idea how to be there in between. And at this point neither do I. The saddest part about all of this is debatable. It is either the inability to fix it or the knowledge that I have no idea what I would be trying to make it if I did try to fix it. Like my sister says, I have nothing to compare it to.

Consequence Based vs. Value Based

I said earlier that narcissists are consequence based and not value based except for the value of getting their ego needs met. So what does this really mean? I remember back in the 70s when I first met Ayn Rand, the author of ATLAS SHRUGGED and THE FOUNTAINHEAD as well as many philosophical treatises. I was spellbound by her forceful personality but especially by her words. One of the things she said that day, which I had read many times before, without hearing and seeing the conviction behind her words, was that values are something we ACT on to gain or to keep. Along those same lines, a friend of mine for many years, used to say 'turn off the sound and watch the movie'.

We can tell a person's values by their actions. If a person says she values honesty while telling untruths, she may value the concept of honesty but she certainly doesn't value being honest. This is true for all values and all people. Just watch the movie. A narcissist will say he or she values whatever you want them to say in order to have you give them what they need. They will not behave according to what they say they value. They will behave in accordance with what they really do value, and yes, that is their own needs.

I remember saying many times through the years that I could not reconcile my then husband's behavior with the love he insisted he had for me. In my mind, it just did not compute. All the words of love did not make me feel loved but the behavior certainly made me feel unloved and my needs unimportant. This is another similarity with the group of those effected by living with and loving a narcissist. They just don't feel loved and cared for.

Being consequence based is easy to explain. Behaviors are taken or not taken depending upon the degree of risk of discovery and how severe they think the consequence might be. This is what keeps them in line. Usually their deceptions are so well thought out and implemented that they believe the risks are small and the gains great enough to take a chance. When it comes to subterfuge, they are quite brilliant, imaginative and often quite convincing in their explanations. Those who love them can either look the other way over and over again or begin to believe everything is their fault or hang on to sanity by their fingernails while falling further and further down the rabbit hole, or they can run for their lives.

I mentioned the late Ayn Rand earlier. I was a student of hers for years. She was a proponent of 'reality'; of Aristotle's law of non-contradiction. A is A..always. Something is either true or it isn't. Something happened or it didn't. As a person who has lived life based on these premises, I must have been a narcissists worst nightmare. I questioned and confronted everything. I could not let something go until it was resolved. However with a narcissist things don't get resolved, ever. Especially if it means they might actually see and learn something about themselves. Years after a certain behavior they may actually say it was wrong, but when you turn off the sound and watch the movie, they will do the same thing again, only the next time they will do it better. It's all calculated to get you to leave them alone and take your confrontation away while still giving them what they need.

If a narcissist's partner has values that do not include seeing and living in an objective reality there are ways to maintain the relationship. It all depends upon what is important to you. As I mentioned before, two somatic narcissists feeding each others egos and not expecting anything deeper or more substantial can go on together forever. If they are both satisfied with the relationship and getting what they need, far be it for anyone to say it is wrong. It is only not enough if you really want to know, understand and completely trust the person you love.

Values are usually consistent over time and chosen by the person through introspection and the desire to be a person of high character and standards. This person values being trusted and esteemed based upon who he or she really is and how he or she navigates through life. These people don't leave a trail of hurt, broken, wounded, angry people behind them. They are not narcissists. If you look at the people the narcissist has left behind that is what you will find.

Everyone eventually winds up calling the one they loved so deeply, 'an ugly person'. I have heard this term over and again from many of those touched by a narcissist. It is not a coincidence. What I found interesting is that I didn't hear the term 'evil' when describing them. Somehow, instinctively we get that they are not evil or even malicious. The word 'ugly' really does seem to fit. Their ugliness is in their cavalier attitude, it is within the mindlessness in which they hurt, deceive and abandon those who love them, it is within the fact that there is no backward glance or second thought to their actions, it is within their total disregard to how you must be feeling.

I heard a story of a man who knew he was breaking up with his girlfriend the very next day because he found someone he believed would love him more and give him more. With full knowledge that he was leaving her, he had sex with her the night before. Then the next day told her he met someone else and was breaking off their relationship. Can you imagine her devastation? Can you imagine her humiliation? Of course she didn't know that the entire time he was dating her, which was many years, he had at least five other women he was dating and having sex with at the same time. One of them even lived in his home and slept in his bed with him for months. And by the way, the new woman had no idea he was having sex with the woman he was breaking up with. She is the one who gave me this story to use. She didn't find this out until after she married him. I personally believe the woman who was left was really the lucky one. The one who married him endured years of pain and anger until he left her for the next one who, of course, he believed would love him even more.

I guess 'ugly' is really the right word. Evil would come from the desire to hurt. I truly don't believe there is a desire to harm anyone. You must understand that there is no 'anyone' to harm. The other person does not exist as an individual with feelings but rather a means to the fulfillment of the narcissist. The other person is an instrument only and when they have served as much purpose as possible or the reverse, actually upset him and make him unhappy, there is no more use for them. The pain caused them is not even up for consideration. They are not consciously choosing to hurt anyone...it just doesn't matter.

Being totally self-referential, the narcissist believes that because he or she is finished with the relationship that you are also and if you aren't yet, you will be soon so it's not a really big deal. Because they are only functioning at that maintenance level they really do believe that everyone else does also. They don't understand that if you are not one of them, you will be devastated. You might have just suffered a severe psychological trauma. You might believe you will never be whole or even functional again. You might have all those physical symptoms I mentioned earlier. You might be on medication to cope. They can't relate to it at all. It's not that they are cruel or sadistic on purpose....they really just don't get it. And while you are going through your own special hell and dealing with what is tantamount to drug withdrawal or post traumatic stress syndrome, the narcissist will be telling you that he wants to be friends. And remember, as you are considering his offer, he never, ever, ever wants you back in the same way you probably still want him.

Being the world's best buddy will not make him fall in love with you. It will just add to the narcissistic supply he so badly needs and you are allowing yourself to be used to satisfy his ego. Please say 'thanks, but I'll pass' and if possible, stop all communication with him. He will not respond to your wonderful, fun personality or your charm and charisma, as he will not respond to your pain or your tears or your physical symptoms. He is done and he has moved on. Please save yourself a lot of additional grief and do whatever you have to to stay away from him.

Understand that you are not taking yourself away in order to manipulate him to get a response from him. That would be useless. He doesn't do anything he really doesn't want to do and your removing yourself from his life is really OK with him because he never really committed to having you in his life anyway. Actually, he doesn't know what commitment means. Even if you were married you probably never really felt the true partnership of marriage.

After your romantic relationship is over, he will look at possible outcomes or consequences for himself. If being out of your life will cause him to lose something he wants, he will continue to try to keep you as a friend. If you turn down the offer of friendship he may try to keep in touch but if you don't respond in short order he will give up and move along especially if there is the possibility of a negative consequence.

Keeping you in his life is not a true value to him, but merely another means for him to possibly receive some of the ego stroking and exoneration he desires.

The Narcissist and Personal Freedom

It is inherent in all human beings to value freedom and in truth we are all free.

We are free because we always have choices. The first line of choice is whether to think or not. The second is, if we choose to think, what will it be about. Our feelings are the result of our thoughts. A 'for me' thought will produce a positive feeling and a 'not for me' thought will produce a negative feeling. If we judge something to be for our lives we will feel good and if against our lives, we will feel bad.

It's as simple as that. These thoughts or judgments of ours often occur out of our awareness. They are automatic and lightening fast so we are left believing that our feelings just came out of the blue unbidden and not understood. But we can always trace them back to our thoughts.

Our third line of choice on the freedom trail is our action. We are free to take whatever actions we want to take. Our fourth line is understanding the consequences of our actions. There's an old saying "take what you want said God, and pay for it". When we are value-based we see going against our own values or ethics as a negative consequence to our feelings of well-being. So we choose our value. But we recognize that there is freedom here. We are free to choose...always. Some people even choose imprisonment or death when it is a choice between that and their values. They know that that is still freedom. They understand that freedom is not having no commitments but rather the choice of what those commitments will be. These people know that even in jail or as a POW they are still free. Think of Nelson Mandela or John McCain to name but two. Their bodies may have been bound but they believed their spirits, the deepest part of themselves, were free.

Contrast that with the definition of freedom held by the narcissist. To him freedom is not having any commitments and is in fact a feeling of having no responsibility to anything but his own feelings and desires and whims. Commitment is a word that sends shivers down his spine.

As a minor example, my husband used to play tennis three mornings a week in a league. They began at 9 AM and rotated players. He didn't 'feel' like being there at 9. He would get there at 9:30 so he could get that extra half hour of sleep. He didn't, to his credit, expect them to hold up playing for him and was happy to be rotated in when he got there. After quite a while of this the other men became irritated and one of them volunteered to call and say that if he wanted to stay in the league he had to arrive at 9 like everyone else. My husband tried all manner of excuses and manipulations without success. When the call ended he had plenty to say about how stupid the rule was and how he should not be subjected to it.

It reminded me of another conversation we had. I play competitive bocce also in a league and wanted him to be my partner. I thought it would be a good way for us to do something together with an air of cooperation rather than the adversarial relationship we had developed. He wouldn't do it because we had a specific schedule to follow and he refused to commit to that because it took away his freedom. He would do certain things at a set time with a group, like kayaking or sailing, because he said if he didn't feel like showing up he didn't have to. He didn't want anyone relying on him because it made him feel trapped (his word).

On a more serious note, I realized in short order that he never committed to being married either. I remember when we were first discussing it and his questions about his freedom were uppermost in his mind He questioned me over and over about what would be acceptable to me for him to do. My answer at the time was the same thing it would be today and that is anything that doesn't entail a romantic or sexual relationship with another woman. I did, however, ask to be advised about what he was doing and where he was going. I naturally told him the same thing about my comings and goings. As it turned out, I was only told things that he thought I wouldn't mind knowing. Anything that he decided I wouldn't like was kept secret.

His idea of freedom was really complete and total irresponsibility. His own words were that he wanted to do anything at any time without having to answer to anyone. I believe that his basic feeling is of not being free within himself. At root it is fear of having to rise to an occasion or come through for someone in some fundamental way and knowing he cannot. Being trapped by his own sense of inadequacy at being an authentic person, it is far easier to drift through life on an emotional level, feeling whatever feelings surface without even knowing the thoughts responsible for them. To not know is to not evaluate. To not evaluate is the narcissists answer to freedom.

So inevitably, I became more and more insecure and felt more and more uncared for and less and less as though I were married. It didn't happen all at once and it didn't happen quickly but somewhere along the way I lost myself in that relationship. And in so doing I tried to change him into someone who could understand what was happening. I figured if I talked long enough and loud enough I could somehow get through to him. He planted his proverbial feet and dug in and wouldn't budge. He wouldn't have anyone telling him what to do. This was a huge issue. It took away his freedom. Not understanding that he was inherently free, he fought against everything I said or did so he could hold on tightly to his illusion of freedom. And on it went until it didn't and he was gone. It couldn't have ended any other way.

Icanseenow,ofcourse,thatthroughmyowninsecurity,I wasattemptingtocurtailhisfreedom.Thisissomething I shamefully admit and a value I would never have believed I could choose or act upon. At the time I wanted some sort of proof that I mattered to him. Since he became my drug and I became addicted I also became as irrational as any addict would at the fear of being cut off from my drug. It became a horrible unbearably painful cycle.

I, who had always considered myself rational and 'free' became neither.

Clarity did not become my partner again, until distance and detox occurred.

Self Esteem and Enlightened Self Interest vs. Narcissism

Before you begin to think that people of authentic self esteem may be narcissists, some definitions are in order and some behaviors need to be explained. The subject of self-esteem comes up quite often in my work with people. Recently I gave a short workshop about the subject and the work of Nathaniel Branden always comes up. His book, THE PSYCHOLOGY OF SELF-ESTEEM was written in 1969 and now, over 40 years later, is still a best seller and the premier book on the subject. Since I've read this book at least 5 times from cover to cover and a multitude of times piecemeal, I can't really separate what he says from what I would say so I will credit

Dr. Branden with this chapter although it is written in my words.

Self-Esteem has two parts to it and they are inherently inter-related. It consists of a sense of personal efficacy along with a sense of personal worth. It means I am competent to live (happily) and worthy of living (happily).

In order to seek to fulfill values that will lead to happiness a person must choose those values volitionally and purposefully. He/she needs to use reasoning abilities to choose correctly but must also value the beneficiary of those values which is him or herself. So in order to seek happiness and person must feel worthy to achieve it.

Self-esteem is a moral appraisal and since morality pertains only to the volitional (that which is open to choice) a person who continually makes choices that lead to pain and misery would be said to have poor reasoning ability or a lack of self-esteem. The first act of volition that leads to self-esteem is the choice to think or to 'fog out', to consciously and deliberately observe and evaluate reality or pretend to not see what you see or know what you know. To be able to understand the consequences of one's choices and not just act without thought to what the probable outcomes of one's behavior will be.

As a person makes appropriate choices leading to success and happiness he or she develops the sense of worth that leads to more appropriate choices and the cycle continues and self-esteem grows. If we like the outcomes we have produced in our lives we achieve a sense of pride in our competency and that leads to feeling worthy of more positive outcomes.

One thing that I would like to make really clear is that self-esteem is not something that comes from the outside or that someone else can bestow upon us. The opinions of others are important in that they are another aspect of the reality that we need to observe and evaluate. If we value another person for his taste, judgment, intelligence, etc. and that person thinks badly of us it is something we must consider but if we do not value those characteristics in someone else what they think of us is irrelevant.

Sometimes a person will possess all the tools necessary for competency and personal success but repeatedly mess up their desired outcomes. When we see this in someone enough times we usually say that person has a 'tragic flaw'. What we mean but often don't know it, is that person does not feel worthy of happiness and success. This is mostly in a particular area of the person's life and rarely in all areas.

Sometimes a person has a pseudo-sense of entitlement and believes he or she should have whatever they want in life. But somehow others can tell that this is not a true sense of self-worth but rather an arrogant sign of just a 'good act'. These people, even when they are successful in their achievements never seem to feel good about it.

This type of person, and I'm sure we all know at least one, actually has extremely low self-esteem, doesn't want to face it and certainly doesn't want anyone else to know it. Their arrogance, boastfulness, self-righteousness and demanding ways (to name a few) are an attempt to overpower and overwhelm others into seeing them as powerful and sure of themselves. Sometimes it actually works when the people they are trying to impress also have low self-esteem but meeker personalities. These people actually do not feel 'right' as a person which basically means that they don't truly feel fit for happiness and therefore run as fast as they can (metaphorically) to avoid the threat of pain, especially the threat of the pain of being found out.

So now, that you know a little about what self-esteem really is, let's look at it in conjunction with the narcissist. To begin, the narcissist has low self-esteem. That is what is partly responsible for the necessary narcissistic supply to keep coming. He or she wrongly believes that having that supply high enough will at some point lead to real feelings of worth and adequacy. However, even that belief is below the surface of consciousness because the narcissist would never even allow those thoughts to enter conscious thinking. He just has the feeling that something out there will make him feel better and as long as it keeps coming, he actually does feel better. The anxiety of having any real negative feelings will be kept at bay as long as the pseudo feelings are there While people of true self-esteem are not ashamed to share their thoughts and feelings, narcissists cannot share themselves at that intimate level because of their fear of being truly seen and then rejected and because they are so pinched off from their inner selves. They know that as 'real' people they haven't much to offer so they develop this outer personality full of charm and fun or achievement that draws the ego-stroking. As long as they don't have to continue the act for too long at a time, they will be fine. This is the main reason they can't have any truly intimate relationships. Sooner or later they will be found out for the shams they really are. Those people who have authentic self-esteem have very little or no fear of being 'found out' so they love having psychological visibility and grow from intimate relationships.

The intellectual narcissist fools people in the self-esteem area more often than the somatic narcissist. The somatic takes his or her worth from the body and physical ability and perhaps their self-esteem is even normal in these areas. But as an entire person with feelings, thoughts, values and character, they have very low self-esteem.

When we meet an intellectual narcissist, he or she is often in a position of power and authority. Remember that is where they get their supply from. They become experts in their field of endeavor and take a leadership role where they have a great deal of influence over others. The supply they desire is admiration and respect.

They don't necessarily need physical affection and they are often not as sensual as the somatic narcissist. Since their authority is often admired and they are looked up to it looks to the outside world as if they have high self-esteem. They may be competent in their abilities but they don't view themselves as deserving as much as they view themselves as entitled. They also, know that under their facades they haven't much to offer. They keep their relationships in the one-up position where they have all the power and others have very little or none at all. They can be as sexual as the somatic narcissist but sex to them entails more power than affection and they are often extremely selfish lovers sometimes even cruel.

Remember that narcissists don't see people as having their own needs and when they pretend to be giving the other person what they need it is because it is calculated to add to their own supply. If they could get the supply without satisfying the partner they most likely would.

People of high self-esteem, of course, are on a path to achieving happiness. Yes, their needs, desires and feelings matter. They seek fulfillment and achievement and think thoughts that make them feel good Do not confuse this with the narcissist to whom no one else really matters. The person of true self-esteem wants everyone to feel as he does and to reach their own aspirations. The narcissist doesn't care. He may care about the masses as a concept but doesn't really concern himself with any other individual particular person. Again, he may do things that allow him to feel good about himself and disprove his lingering dread that he is not all that involved with others but it will be strictly to relieve his own discomfort.

Selfishness vs. Enlightened Self-Interest

Selfishness has a bad reputation so although I am not against selfishness in general, I'm going to use it here as narcissistic selfishness and refer to the positive type of selfishness as enlightened or rational self-interest.

With enlightened self-interest, a person's needs are important and the person finds ways to meet them. Living in a world full of people who are rationally looking to fulfill themselves is a benefit to the environment. If I were a person of rational self-interest, I would prefer living in a clean environment. I would prefer living in a healthy environment. I would prefer living in a happy environment. I would prefer living in a crime-free environment. I would prefer living in a drug-free environment. I would prefer living in a poverty free environment. I think you can see where this is leading. If these things were important to me I would do my best to bring them about. I may be concentrating on my own needs but ultimately I would be bringing about a better world for everyone. Imagine if all those other people also lived in that way. Because their self-interest is rational and enlightened, they too, would find themselves attempting to bring about the best world possible for themselves to live in.

Contrast that with the narcissist whose only 'selfish' interest is getting his own supply fulfilled. He doesn't and can't fulfill himself in these areas. Instead, he wants you to do it for him. Of course, if asked, he would also want to live in the above described universe but he is still and only concerned with himself in the moment. His choices are made more through whims and immediate desire than long range, local and/or global interest based on values and true aspirations.

Just for clarification, his needed narcissistic supply is not in all areas of life. There are many areas in which he is quite balanced and can think long-term, rationally and responsibly. It is only within the parameters in which he finds himself psychologically, emotionally and/or spiritually inadequate that the narcissism is evident and he uses others to satisfy his needs.

This chapter seems like the best place to put the next few words about the 'isms': egoism, altruism, egotism, narcissism. What do they all mean?

Egoism and altruism are basically philosophical orientations that have been argued for years. Altruism is supposedly valuing and behaving with the needs of the 'other' coming before one's own and egoism is its opposite. I remember writing a term paper in college arguing that there is no such thing as altruism because all deeds ultimately collapse into what feels best to the doer and most meets those values which would make them acts of egoism. My professor wrote that although he disagreed with me philosophically, based on my argument he couldn't find fault with the logic. I received an A.

I still believe that people cannot act deliberately contrary to their own values and well-being. Even the act of suicide is an attempt to remove oneself from a situation deemed worse than death. An egoist will act with rational self-interest as described above.

An egotist is someone we regard as ego-centric, vain or conceited. Unlike narcissists, egotists seem really to know, like and respect themselves. They haven't a problem sharing their thoughts and feelings with others and are honest about their lives. They seem to be aware of their strengths and want to work hard on their weaknesses. They are probably also egoists in the philosophical sense.

Marielle

I met Marielle in the dining car of an Amtrak train to Atlanta about 12 years ago. I judged her to be in her mid forties. She was very attractive and intelligent. We began with chit-chat and realized we were both taking the train rather than flying for the same reasons. Neither of us really liked flying but the main reason was to have some quality time with ourselves to read, write and reflect. Marielle asked what I did and I told her I was a psychotherapist. At that she offered to buy me dinner if she could pick my brain (as she put it). Of course I said she didn't have to buy me dinner, I would gladly listen and if I could help, I would. She insisted and I accepted. Here is the story she told me.

She married in her late twenties and divorced about five years later. There were no children from that marriage. During the next six years she dated quite a bit, had a few long term relationships but never met anyone she wanted to marry. Until seven years ago when she met Roger. She was 39, he was 45 and had been divorced for over ten years. His former wife was killed in an automobile accident about two years prior to their meeting. He had two sons, 19 and 21 and both attended Notre Dame.

Marielle met Roger when she was applying for the position of Vice President of Advertising at his company. It was to be the final interview. If the President/CEO approved, the job was hers. About half-way through the interview Roger said he hadn't eaten all day and was very hungry and invited her to accompany him for lunch which she did. She told me he was very appropriate throughout the lunch, telling her how proud he was of the company he started and explaining to her how it all came about. She was sincerely impressed and said so. When lunch was over he reached across the table, took her hand, and said she couldn't have the job because he was going to marry her and it wouldn't look good to the employees. Her thought was that there were plenty of jobs out there but only one man like Roger. He was successful, smart, and handsome. What else could a woman possibly wish for?

The next few months were a whirlwind of activities......all chosen by Roger. They went to the theater, ballet, opera, museums, art galleries and the best restaurants that served the food that Roger preferred. Marielle believed she was getting the best education in culture that New York had to offer. She didn't allow herself to dwell on the times she wanted to see a silly movie and have a pizza. She would do those things with a girlfriend. She believed herself to be the luckiest woman alive.

After a year she noticed that their sex life had changed. He was now the one to set the time and if he wasn't in the mood nothing she ever did could change that. He began to be more controlling and inconsiderate of her needs. He also began to 'teach' her more ways to please him without reciprocating. But, Marielle said sadly, the worst part was that he didn't really seem to care whether they made love or not or cuddled afterward or not or even if she were there or not. When she mentioned that they should think about living together, he told her he wasn't ready. He seemed happiest when he was impressing her with his intellect, money, knowledge and success and she was showing him how much she appreciated those attributes in him. At other times, if she didn't want to be the student and in fact wanted to show him her own competencies he became withdrawn and aloof.

I then stopped her discourse to ask what she was feeling and why she stayed with him when it was obvious to me that she wasn't being fulfilled in important areas.

She said all this was in retrospect and she wasn't unhappy in those earlier years with him. She told me she had believed she had found her ideal partner and that she herself must either be lacking or unappreciative of all she had. After all, Roger was perfect, knew so much about so much, had great successes in business. How could she ever complain about him? The fact that her closest friends and family didn't like him and could not ever get close to him did not move her into giving him another evaluation. She said she was still too much in awe of him.

During the second year of their relationship she met his sons. They were respectful towards Roger but did not seem to exude any warmth towards him nor he towards them. The time spent together was pleasant but not really enjoyable. Roger spent a lot of time asking his boys questions about school and their plans for the future. To Marielle it seemed very formal and forced but when she mentioned it to Roger he gave her a lecture about the appropriateness of his relationship with his sons and how she could not possibly understand a parent/child relationship since she had no children of her own. Marielle did not 'interfere' again. After that incident, however, she started to recall other times when Roger alluded to her not being able to understand something he was telling her. Since he had no interest in her areas of expertise she never got the chance to show him the things she was capable of.

I asked about his apparent hold over her and what it felt like. She told me she felt mesmerized by him; by his competency, success and charm. When she thought of breaking it off with him, she felt frightened and alone and realized she had come to depend upon Roger for his parent-like care of her and by the pride she felt that he had chosen her to be with. He would seem almost grateful as well when she told him how much she appreciated him, respected him and needed him. She realized that when she told him she loved him, it didn't get nearly the same kind of response.

After the fourth year of 'dating' Roger said he would allow Marielle to move in with him. That seemed to be when the real problems began. Roger didn't like it when she wasn't spending her time concentrating on him. If she were reading a book, he would inspect the cover to see what it was and what it was about. If it was a novel, he told her she was wasting her time. If it was non-fiction, it was always a subject he found plebeian or nonsensical. If she watched a movie at home, it was always something he found beneath his intelligence and told her it should be beneath hers as well. He never wanted to sit with her or be romantic. He didn't like to be touched if it wasn't about sex. The only time he seemed really happy was when he was teaching her something and she was a grateful student. If Marielle wanted to have a discussion about her feelings or the state of their relationship he would put her off saying everything was fine.

Then about six months ago while shopping in a department store she met a woman who worked for Roger's company. They decided to get a cup of coffee and the woman asked if the bank loan for the business had come through. Not wanting to say that she knew nothing about a bank loan, Marielle said she didn't think so. Thinking then, that Marielle knew what was happening in the business, the woman went on to spill a few other 'secrets'.

Right after that, one of Roger's sons came to visit. He had graduated a few years earlier and moved to California. He was in NY on business. Roger wasn't yet home so Marielle let the son, Rick, in and they talked for a while. Rick mentioned that he went to school on a full scholarship as did his brother. Marielle was shocked. Roger had told her how much it had cost him to put the boys through school. She didn't tell Roger either thing she discovered. Instead she began to pry through his bank statements and receipts and yes, she found many discrepancies between what he told her and what the records showed.

Why was he lying to her? Could she trust or believe him? Was it really her business since they were not married? Did she even want to marry him now? Why was she still staying with him and most importantly why did it scare her so much to even consider leaving the relationship? She told me she felt 'addicted' to him and could not face the pain of withdrawal. She was now in an almost constant state of anxiety wondering what was true and what wasn't. She didn't think he lied about anything that didn't involve money and status but she couldn't be sure. Maybe she just hadn't found out yet. She couldn't show her awe of him like she used to and he became more and more demanding of her admiration and less and less affectionate and complimentary to her. He disregarded her opinions and degraded her tastes and preferences and yet she still couldn't leave.

As we talked and as I asked her questions about her own dwindling self-esteem, it appeared as though she were coming to a decision.

Marielle and I kept in touch for about a year. It took months for their relationship to collapse and for Roger to insist she move out because she was no longer meeting his needs and he believed she no longer 'respected' him. She then relocated to Seattle where she slowly regained her sense of self after that very traumatic break-up. Looking back it is obvious that Roger was an Intellectual Narcissist.

Being Self-Referential

The narcissist sees everything only through his or her point of view. Yes, most people do, but most people CAN, when asked, put themselves into another's position and see an experience from the other's eyes The narcissist can't. Everything that is experienced is somehow related to them.

I remember a few years ago my husband and I were driving to NYC. We lived close to 150 miles from there and got on the Garden State Parkway in very south New Jersey close to Atlantic City. There was quite a bit of traffic and he said there were a lot of people going to NYC that day and he wondered why. I wondered why he would think that they were going there at all. After all we were two and a half hours away and those cars could have been going anywhere. Then we saw two cars up ahead that were obviously traveling together. When one would change lanes so would the other. He then commented that they must be two brothers with one following the other. I asked why he thought they were two brothers (of course, knowing the answer). I said they could have any kind of relationship. He seemed taken aback and surprised by my comment because he never considered that. You already must have guessed that he has a brother so that was what came to mind.

These are minor, silly examples but with the narcissist life is all about examples like these. They cannot see past their own experience and the disorder prevents them from being able to see both sides of any situation. The only time it may appear as though they understand what another person may be experiencing is if it is very much like their own. Otherwise it is completely foreign and they don't care enough to make an attempt at getting it. Because of this, they often choose partners they believe see life and enjoy similar activities as they do. Often you see a narcissist with someone who is the mirror image of themselves. When they partner up with someone with wide differences in preferences, enjoyments and values the conflicts loom large and the relationship fails, usually quickly.

Although most people enjoy being with someone compatible, the narcissist is often threatened by differences. A person who is similar is more comfortable because the narcissist feels safer and never has to look at the alternative viewpoint. This also guarantees that there is no personal growth or spiritual evolution because there is no contrast. Since the narcissist actually feels quite bad about him or herself, being with someone of like mind or orientation ensures that the judgments will be more favorable.

I remember that when trying to relate an emotion I was feeling to my husband, I always attempted to bring in physical descriptions because that was the only level at which he could relate. I would scan my body noticing physical tensions and sensations. Since I knew he could understand rapid heartbeats and stomach knots, those would be easy to relate. I tried to keep away from all psychologically worded descriptions although those would have been easier for me. I knew there wasn't much of a basis of communication using those types of phrases.

He was always more understanding and helpful if I were physically ill with a cold or sore throat or if

I were injured in some way like a bruise or sprain, than he could ever have been if I were suffering emotionally. (which I usually was). That seemed to be foreign territory unless it was an emotion he had experienced under similar circumstances. Only if it happened within his experience did it ever have any relevancy.

Many years ago, when I wasn't even 30 yet, I learned a form of communication of feelings that I found very enlightening. When an issue or a topic was brought up I would write about my feelings regarding it and when I believed I had made myself clear, I would have it read by the other person and then we would speak about it in an attempt to convey even greater understanding of the feelings in question. When the focus was on the other person's feelings the exercise was done in reverse. It was an intimate exercise and one in which we would feel closer and more psychologically visible. Contrast this with attempting to make yourself known to a narcissist or worse attempting to see and understand the narcissist. It would be a very frustrating exercise in futility as they cannot see things from another's point of view and are uncomfortable

sharing their own feelings. But I kept trying.

Emotional Currency

Everyone has ways in which they want to get paid emotionally or intimately. These are the behaviors, gestures, etc. that lead to a person feeling loved, valued, appreciated and a host of other psychological necessities. Different people use different currencies to give and receive closeness and impart feelings of caring and love.

For example, service. Both men and women use service to show their love. A woman may pick up her husband's shirts at the cleaners and he may wash her car. If both people view service in the same way, they both will feel loved and cared for when these favors are done for them. However, if one of them just regards doing these things as part of running a household, that person will not feel 'paid' by the gesture. Oftentimes the other will point this out and say he or she felt unappreciated when the overture was met with a mere 'thanks' because the partner on the receiving end thought it was not particularly special.

Another example is money or gifts. Sometimes one partner believes that buying an extravagant gift is a wonderful way of showing love. If the person on the receiving end thinks the same way, then both partners will feel loved and appreciated and their emotional banks will have a deposit. If, however, you have one partner believing that gifts are a show of love and the other partner thinking that picking up the dry cleaning is, we're going to have two unfulfilled people. The one who didn't receive the gift and the one whose trip to the cleaners was not appreciated. Neither partner here is going to feel emotionally paid.

One very important difference is in what constitutes emotional intimacy. I'll use myself for the next example. To me, closeness comes from intimate conversation. These conversations can be intellectual as well as emotionally revealing. They come from sharing ideas, philosophies, theories, experiences and opinions as well as intimate and personal feelings. This is true for me in any relationship whether it's with friends, my daughters, spouse, etc. This was also true when I ran groups and watched people blossom because they were able to share their deepest selves and their ideas and learn to accept the sharings of others. For me, this is what it means to be 'in relationship' with another person and this is what fosters intimacy and love for another.

You must now be chuckling to yourselves wondering how I wound up in love with a narcissist for whom intimate sharing is the last method of emotional payment he would ever partake in. So when I am not getting paid in a way that matters to me, I can only reach a certain level of relationship. This may be fine in casual friendships and acquaintanceships but those relationships cannot deepen. Of course I also tend to pay in that same currency and although I can and do pay in all forms of emotional currency they are not primary for me.

So I can have a good mental relationship (I will discuss this also) with a cerebral narcissist but it will never turn into an intimate relationship. As you can probably tell, a relationship with a somatic narcissist would have been basically impossible until and unless my currency changed or was redirected.

Another important currency is time. Some people require spending a great deal of time with the other and some need much less. If you believe that the amount of time spent together should be a primary factor of the relationship, being with someone with many other interests who doesn't have the same time requirements you do will make you both unhappy. You will see the time spent doing other things as a rejection of you and the other person will find your demands suffocating and neither of you will be filling your bank.

Time spent together is definitely an important factor in relationships. It is difficult to feel loved and cared for when the person you want to be with hasn't the time to spend with you. But the important thing to look at here is desire. If the other person has a time-consuming job or other necessary demands to meet but you know you are valued and the desire to spend the time with you is there, it is quite different than being with someone who is fitting you in to a whimsical schedule. A narcissist fits that latter category. He will see you when he feels like it and will feel pressured when you want to see him if it doesn't meet his immediate needs. Remember, he wants no type of demand put on him.

If you are in love with a person who finds it difficult or impossible to pay you with your primary emotional currency you can find other methods of payment that together fill your 'bank' and receive your main currency from other relationships or you can decide that you will be unhappy with someone, regardless of your feelings for them, without receiving it and then it is only fair and compassionate to move on. Trying to receive something from someone who is unable to give it is a major effort in frustration and futility for both of you.

Another method of payment, that works well for the somatic narcissist is paying with physical affection and/or compliments and flattery. Since that is the narcissists life blood it will be very important for you to give and the narcissist to receive. It is normal and natural for everyone to want to give and receive affection but for the somatic narcissist it is for the most part singularly important and plays the primary role in the relationship. He or she will willingly give you the same thing because it will lead to them receiving it. As I said earlier, it is a behavior that is not primarily aimed at you, but at themselves.

To be paid in your own currency is to experience yourself as loved, valuable, important, cared for, psychologically visible and a real part of a relationship. To be paid in a way that is less important to you or even in a way you might not notice, leads to feeling invisible as your deepest self and when you feel invisible you naturally cannot feel loved and cared for. Imagine how you feel when your emotional currency bank is empty or you even experience it as a deficit versus having an EC bank that is overflowing.

One of the themes of people involved in relationship with a narcissist is that they do not feel as though their EC bank is filling up and they are emotionally exhausted. Most of the time they don't know exactly what is happening. They only feel drained and tired after the initial high has gone. The only kind of person who can remain feeling fulfilled is another person who has the same emotional currency as the narcissist. Since they are completely self-referential they will be able to give you what you need as long as they need the same thing and understand it and can be assured of reciprocation. So realize that if your emotional currency needs are different than either type of narcissist you will never have them met.

There are two other categories of emotional currency that I would like to mention because they have direct impact on life with the narcissist.

The first one is Flattery and Compliments. If these are genuine and not manipulative they can go a long way in filling your EC bank. However, it is rare that these fit into that category with the narcissist. You will be flattered when it suits him or her to do so to get what they want. Since you are not a real person anyway, the flattery and compliments aren't real either. Their opposites; insults and criticism empty the EC bank much more quickly than flattery and compliments can fill them. It is often said that it takes a thousand genuine compliments to undo a single hurtful insult and the narcissist is quite quick to criticize and insult. It will become more and more difficult for you to want to fill his EC bank while he is depleting yours and the cycle will most likely begin to spiral downward because while he is not getting his bank filled he will become more and more verbally abusive and you will become more and more loathe to compliment him and give him the affection he so badly needs.

The last category to mention is more of an orientation or state of being. I think it might be the single most important factor in having a good relationship and the narcissist is incapable of it. It is loyalty, honesty and trust. Without these, you can have all the above mentioned categories and have a working partnership to a degree but you can never have an intimate relationship because there can never be psychological intimacy and visibility. If this is important to you and you believe it to be the mainstay of the relationship you are looking for, realize it can never be with anyone with NPD.

I believe emotional currency is a very important and overlooked facet of relationships and the more you understand your own needs, the more you can measure what you are receiving against what it is that grows your own soul and your own interactions whether they are romantic or simply friendships or family interactions. A relationship with a narcissist can never lead you to become a more mature or better person and it can certainly not enhance your connection to your inner being. You will have to do that yourself, which is doable but how much nicer to share it with someone you love.

The more you understand yourself and your own needs and priorities, you can then decide for yourself if continuing your relationship with a narcissist can bring you any kind of pleasure or satisfaction.

For me, no matter what my feelings for my husband were, I was not able, at that time, to deal with his NPD on a continuing basis without losing myself.

Perhaps the next chapter will give you another insight into what you are looking for in a relationship so you can make your choices with more clarity.

Levels of Relationship

I'm only calling these levels for lack of a better description. Feel free to put your own perspective on them.

Let's call the first level that of the physical because it takes place only in the material/physical universe and work our way up to the soul level where there is a great deal of spirituality involved. These categories pertain to all types of relationships as did the chapter on emotional currency but when it is a sexual or romantic relationship sexual functioning most likely coincides with the level of the rest of the interactions the couple engages in.

On the physical level of a relationship (the one the somatic narcissist will relate mostly to), the people enjoy doing things together a d are said to be living in their bodies in the world of 'things'. They relate to the world and to each other on this plane. They are tuned in to their bodily senses and are highly sensitive to pleasure and pain. Of course, they try to have as much physical pleasure as possible and they weigh their activities by that measurement.

Their idea of fun is that which feels good at that very basic level. They enjoy physical activity more than the other orientations. All of us function at this level some of the time. There are always people with whom we like doing things and enjoy the time together sharing these activities. These are sometimes called Activity Partners. Nothing needs to be added to this to allow us to have a satisfying experience. In a sexual/romantic relationship at this level, sex is often also about the experience of two bodies. If the two bodies view each other as attractive and compatible, nothing else is necessary. Sometimes in this category the people may not even have to know each others' names and other times the relationships moves on to a 'no strings attached' sexual relationship.

Without moving 'up' to at least an emotional relationship it is unlikely for this pairing to go any further. Often when a narcissist is involved in a major or primary relationship this type of purely physical one will become a satellite one for however long it is serving its purpose.

On this next level, emotions are also involved. Whatever they may be doing there is more going on than just the physical. So instead of only enjoying the physical sensations of the experience they are bringing in the feelings they are also having. Here they are also dealing with the meaning that the activity has for them. In a sense they are still living in their bodies because that is where the emotions are felt but the experience is becoming wider and more meaningful.

When two people are involved at this level there is more of a sense of relating to another person and not just to another body. The experience is one of feeling more connected and there are feelings of fondness and perhaps even true affection. Since narcissism is on a continuum there are some who can experience a relationship like this. This is what they would refer to as their primary one and they definitely care to some degree about the person but it is usually because they are getting their own emotional needs met as well as their purely physical ones.

Before I write about the spiritual or soul level, I want to say something about the mental level of relationships. These are the types you usually find the intellectual or cerebral narcissist involved in but with them it is not based on equality. They want to find someone who doesn't know as much as they do but still respects the orientation of the intellectual. This level is usually built on common ideas and goals. The interactions can be extremely intense and passionate but the intensity and passion are aimed at and focused on the ideas and not necessarily the other person or people. Most of us have people in our lives with whom we love to discuss politics or religion or economics or any other topic. The discussions are often very heated and we feel totally immersed in them. Sometimes a romantic relationship is begun because of this, but it usually doesn't last unless the ideas keep coming. With the narcissist it won't last unless you remain in awe of them and their knowledge.

The passion of the concepts is often confused with passion for the person. Usually, however, strong friendships are built here or strong enemies are made. Mind-to-mind relationships can be very exciting and very stimulating. When they are mixed with the other categories of relationship and the people have the ability to go back and forth among levels, I believe it can be very powerful. (as long as it is not with an intellectual narcissist)

On the spiritual level people are connected at the soul level. If you believe that we are made up of our bodies, our minds, our feelings and our souls then the soul level can be extremely profound. Here you realize that we are all more than we appear to be. If you believe that the physical body is temporary and the soul is eternal then we know that at that level something continues. When people have that sense of each other they relate differently. Of course at this time, this is belief and theory only although with the discovery of quantum physics this may eventually find a place in science.

I don't know how many people have met someone and felt the distinct connection that can only come from soul-to-soul. The feeling is usually immediate that you have know this person forever. There is something so familiar about this stranger and you just don't know why. Sometimes it's a bad feeling and you just want to run away and never see that person again and sometimes you feel safe and comfortable immediately. If this has never happened to you, then you will most certainly not know what I'm referring to but if it has, then conversely you certainly will. There are different levels of this as well. You may feel a lesser degree of familiarity or feel so connected that you believe you've met a part of yourself in someone else's body.

However, don't view this as the ultimate relationship because you may not be able to relate to or even stand this person in the 'real' world. These people may or may not share values, likes, dislikes, passions, interests or even a preference for the same weather. Just because you feel a deep connection to someone doesn't mean you were meant to share your life or even your home with this person. And then again, sometimes it may mean just that, but not for the obvious reasons.

Sometimes there are lessons we need to learn that only that particular person can teach us and although it might be tumultuous we wind up better people for having learned it....or we don't understand the lesson, never learn it and just wind up hurt and angry. The term soul mate does not necessarily mean someone with whom you have a romantic relationship but rather someone who, because of them, your soul can grow. This might be the most difficult of all our relationships especially when the lessons are unseen and ignored.

If you can be aware of these levels and how they influence your interactions you might get a better feel for how you are relating and the positive and negative experiences in your life.

Most of the partners of narcissists that I have met have referred to the spiritual level in how they feel about the person they are involved with. That is one of the reasons I felt compelled to include this chapter and the one on spirituality. I don't know if all the talk about soul connections is the partner's way of justifying staying with the narcissist or an added dimension to the partnership. Sometimes it sounds as though they are talking about karma or divine intervention. Often they have given over the responsibility for the relationship to a 'higher power' and have convinced themselves that they are supposed to be there, maybe even to rescue the narcissist from his or her empty life. Even if this is true somehow and there is a bigger picture that we aren't seeing, when you shine the light of consciousness on the relationship and all you see is your own pain, anger and frustration, please wonder if this is what you were meant to have in your life and why you would even think that.

Since I have a very strong spiritual orientation I do believe that he and I have a soul connection, but I do not believe that I should be wasting another day of my life in sorrow. If he has an empty life in that bigger picture world, he is just fine with it and it is not my job to convince him otherwise. It is also not yours.

It took me quite a few years to figure that out and when the time came to act on what I had known for a long time, I also didn't want to do it. I couldn't carry out my own decision to leave. Whether it was the soul connection, real deep abiding love, merely the addiction or my own fear of changing my life I could not do it. I am in complete sympathy with what you are going through and maybe my own story, which follows will help you do what you know is right for yourself.

So what do I consider the 'ideal' level of relationship? Again this is strictly a personal perspective and may not apply to anyone but myself. For me the relationship would be growing; both emotionally, spiritually and intellectually. It would be one where both people are striving to be the best they can be and are open to learning new concepts and willing to share themselves with each other. Don't get me wrong, I'm 100% for having fun and being romantic and joyful. All seriousness is not a good thing for any relationship or any individual. In fact

I think 'serious' is a word that some people use to describe a heavy pervasive, negativity. This is not at all the way I am using the word. Using it that way takes all the bliss out of life. Life does not have to be mindless fun vs. heavy seriousness.

Growth is a different concept altogether. What it means to me is that I use my life experience to become more integrated, more in touch with who I am both as a physical human being and as a spiritual entity. It means I pay attention to what is happening in and around me. It means I am connected to my self, my surroundings and other people in a way that broadens my experience and that in a love relationship I want to share that experience with my lover and have him share his with me. When two people grow together it is like a gestalt where the total experience is greater than the mathematical sum of the components. This is truly being in relationship with another person but when it is with someone you deeply love, there can be nothing greater.

Me

In her book, ENCHANTED LOVE, Marianne Williamson has a passage that brings me to tears almost every time I read it. She writes "sometimes if we're very lucky, a hand is laid upon us which has the power, by its very touch, to claim us for its own. Someone has put a stake on our emotional ground. We can love another but not belong to another. Once we know to whom we belong, nothing changes what we know". That stake was put on my emotional ground when I was a mere 13 years old and through the years I learned that yes, I could love another, even deeply and passionately and ongoing, but that special part of my inner being could never belong to anyone else.

I fell in love with a beautiful smile, dreamy eyes, thick black hair and the sexiest arms I could imagine at that innocent age. He was almost 14 and my soul was his forever. Unfortunately.

I don't think he was a full-blown narcissist back then, although his nickname in Junior High School was 'The Peacock'. He was the original Fonzie from Happy Days, with his comb and swagger. But I felt depth and substance. I felt caring. I felt concern and I felt love. Most of all I felt authenticity. He talked and I listened; I talked and he listened. But the relationship took a strange turn two years later. Because of the differences in our backgrounds in what my parents believed were very important areas they wanted us separated. We would not give each other up and so my family moved away. A drastic step, indeed. Everyone who knew us then and still knows us to this day, believe that had that Romeo and Juliet event not taken place we would have phased ourselves and each other out and gone our separate ways. I am not so sure. He was my first love and the one who held my heart and soul. I never doubted at that time that we would reunite and marry.....We did 40 years later.

His previous marriage ended ten years prior to our meeting and he swore he would never marry again.

He told me he felt trapped (there's that word again) the very next day following his marriage. There were red flags waving in front of my eyes that I refused to see. I would not allow myself to even contemplate being wrong for almost my entire life. I had always been one of those people I described as wanting to see and understand what I then called reality. I was one of those people who would always choose thought over hazy sub-consciousness. I was one of those people with a natural accurate insight into people. And then I wasn't. It was that easy.

I was overwhelmed with the idea of the fantasy coming true. I lived a few feet off the ground surrounded by a golden light of love. I felt blessed by the universe. Who needed or wanted reality. I was totally blind. But in the early days I was happier than I had ever been. Maybe I was the one who should have ignored 'reality' and stayed where I was because after six months I began to see what I never wanted to see.

The first big deception occurred three months into our relationship but it would be another three months before I found out that I was lied to. I knew then that I should leave but I was much too enmeshed in the miracle of our being together. He 'explained' the lie and although it took its toll on me I let it go and stayed. After all, the event happened five years before we got together. I did become hypervigilent however, which did neither of us any good.

This is when the addiction/heartache/withdrawal/ addiction/heartache/withdrawal cycle began. I would still at that time, not admit to know what I suspected. I actually married him and I was actually happy. Very happy. Ecstatically happy. For a while. I admit that living in that space of golden light was a lot better and a lot happier than the various 'realities' to come.

The next deception was much more painful and once again I 'tried' to leave and once again I didn't. I don't think I recovered from that one for the rest of the time we were married. I was rightfully mis-trusting and suspicious but I believe now that when you reach that point you must end the relationship for the sake of both people. If you are to become the positive person you want to be, you can't do it while still in that relationship facing the same issues with the same person. It doesn't seem possible to fix a broken relationship from the inside. Time and distance seems to be necessary to evaluate yourself and what you really want.

Now, I have actually come full circle in the way I look at things. I have decided that I really am much happier when I focus on the positive aspects of people and experiences and ignore the negative. I try not to concentrate on things I don't like, but rather look at what I do like. I even have a notebook that I titled Positive Aspects and whenever a situation arises or a person comes into my life I write all the positive aspects I can find. I never write about the negatives. I read over the lists I've written until I know them by heart and they have my attention. I've noticed when I do that I am oriented towards facing things with a hopeful attitude and a loving heart.

Unfortunately what happened in my relationship was that the negative things I was finding back then took all my attention and I then found myself looking for them more and more. I no longer saw anything that would make me feel happy or loving. I was afraid of feeling or seeming foolish. I was afraid of being taken advantage of in some way. Once I realized I had been betrayed or deceived, that was all I could see. I'm not judging whether that was good or bad, right or wrong. What I am saying is that because of that orientation I became a very unhappy and very angry person. From that point on there was nowhere my marriage could have gone except to divorce court. I'm also not saying that it should not have wound up there. I am saying that being hurt and angry did not do me any good personally. In looking back I see that I could have seen the positive side of him and the relationship while at the same time realizing that it was not ultimately the kind of marriage I could be happy in or changed my own focus and chosen to accept him the way he was. There is no blame here, just an understanding of the differences in people and what they each find important and how they want to live their lives.

As for me and my story of loving a narcissist, this is how it is as of this writing. Remember, this is personal to me and certainly not a template for anyone else to compare their own experience to.

Earlier I said I was a narcissists worst nightmare. That was true but as I've grown and dealt with and come through my own private hell, I can see that in one way I may have become a narcissists true fantasy. That is because I can see him clearly; I know the deep negative feelings that are true at the core of his disorder. I also believe that he would be astonished to hear this because he sees himself as happy and his life as full. I know who he really is and I know how he got there. And on a strictly feeling level I love him completely, unconditionally and eternally. My love has only deepened since knowing this....but it is mixed with a sense of sadness. This, too, will surprise him but I see his life as fundamentally sad and empty and this distresses me. I want so much more for him. But what I want for him is based on my own values and my own orientation towards the meaning of life. If they are not his values and he sees and experiences life differently that is who he is and I can only live my own life. When the day comes when I no longer want anything different for him than he wants for himself I will know I have reached a very high level of accepting.

But my thoughts about him and my behavior towards him bear no resemblance to what I thought or how I acted in the past. I think of him as a limited, even damaged person who lives to have one fun sensual experience after another; someone who believes feeling good and satisfying his surface needs are more important than growth and true intimacy; someone to whom emotional safety is more important than honesty and trust, someone who would prefer casual relationships to one where there is two-way commitment and deep love and I do accept all of that. I just don't want to be married to it.

As for my behavior, I took my own advice and I ran from the offer of 'friendship'. When the marriage ended, I preferred no interaction at all. I preferred no contact at all. I preferred to never see his face or hear his voice. I removed all physical traces of him from my surroundings. There is not a single picture in any frame or album. I treated him as an addiction. If I were an alcoholic I would not live with liquor bottles. I made dealing with this loss the top priority in my life by removing any and all triggers that might cause me pain. I am committed to my own growth, spirituality, health and happiness. I intend to build my relationships on trust and honesty or not have any. I am a much different person now. I am a much better person now. In my own very personal way I am thankful for the experience.

I remember throughout the 40 years of separation when I would look at a picture of the teenage boy I fell so deeply in love with and wish to see him 'one more time', to touch him 'one more time', to hold him 'one more time'. I thought I would be satisfied forever if my prayer came true. So I ask myself if knowing then what I know now, would I still have chosen the last 10 years and I think I would. Love is funny that way. Had I not done it, I'd still be wishing for that last 'one more time'. (which actually I am still wishing for and most likely always will be)

A while back, while spending a sleepless night, I had a revelation. I knew without doubt that in my own personal value system, based on my own hierarchical priorities, it was much more important to me that he was happy (even by his narcissistic standards) than that he was with me. Because of that thought I realized that I was truly at peace myself and this my friends is what I wish for you. I will write more about this in the chapter following spirituality.

But, as I sit at my computer writing this section I know that in three weeks I will be seeing him again after seven months. We will be spending two weeks living in the same house. I will write about the experience when it has passed. I'm sure it will be another milestone for me. If I hadn't promised to include my own story in this book I wouldn't be adding what will follow but I believe it will be another step in my own growth and hopefully the readers' as well. As I've written, I believe and support total avoidance of the former narcissistic partner after the relationship is over. Unfortunately this co-habitation cannot be helped. I certainly do not advise it.

Some professionals believe NPD can be changed. I am not one of them. Although I understand their theories I think they are unrealistic. If the threat of loss is too great a narcissist may attempt change but it will be short lived because as soon as the consequence of loss is eased the desire to change will also ease. I think that is just the way it is and I refer the reader to the work of Robert Fritz for a more extensive explanation. A narcissist may be able to change and grow if he really wants to as a value and aspiration, but if he had these, would be really be a narcissist to begin with? I can't answer this since I've never seen it happen.

The Narcissist and Spirituality

The heading of this section may appropriately be called oxymoronic or mutually exclusive. I don't believe there is such a thing as a spiritually oriented narcissist. To my way of thinking any person who sees themselves and others as spiritual beings as well as flesh and blood humans, knows that there is much more to people than the physical or even the physical and mental, which covers both narcissistic types.

A spiritual person must by extension see others as real and individual people with their own needs, feelings, passions and the like. They cannot see others merely as suppliers of their own needs; they cannot see others as existing simply to serve them. It is impossible.

Also, if they believe in the non-physical part of humans, they must realize that this part is connected to an energy they cannot see and that they also have the greater part of themselves made up of this same energy. Let's call it the soul or the energy source or the non-physical or spiritual part. You can use whatever term you feel most comfortable with. Do you think a narcissist gives much thought to that portion of themselves or do you think he rather goes through life wondering what would give him the most immediate sensual pleasure or the best feel-good experience, or the greatest ego-trip? Do you think he cares about spiritual growth or connecting to that which is best or purest or even most powerful within himself? Do you think he gives any attention to the spiritual dimension or asks himself about a higher purpose?

To the somatic narcissist life is about the pleasures of the body, to the cerebral narcissist it is about believing in his intellectual superiority. Both have at root, a sense of emptiness, insecurity and shame. A person with a spiritual connection cannot have those same feelings at their core. They know from where they came and they know what is truly important and where to look for personal growth. The narcissist has no connection to those feelings at all. In fact everything they do is in order to run from ever seeing their core because they believe what they find there will bring the entire facade crumbling down around them. They are very frightened and that's the last thing they ever want to acknowledge. So because they have to go through life hiding that emotional core first, they never get to the spiritual.

I said earlier in this book that this country is not a good place for the aging narcissist. Part of the reason is because many people begin to look at and connect with the spiritual side of themselves after reaching a mature age or having experienced an event that made them question the meaning of life. When they begin to understand and listen to the non-physical within them often they find a deep sense of peace and understanding that carries them through life's tougher trials. The narcissist doesn't get to do this.

When the somatic loses his physical capacities or good looks, or sharpness of mind, it is met with despair because he never developed his person (physical or non). In this country, wonderful as it is, youth and beauty is what is revered and the narcissist, as he ages, becomes out of step and lost. Without another sense of purpose that doesn't rely on physical attributes life becomes as empty as the black hole from which he has been running all his life.

Even the cerebral narcissist is not as honored and esteemed in older age as he was in his youth. He has an easier time than the somatic but this youth oriented country will not put him on the same pedestal or do his bidding as it did in earlier years. Although still respected for his intellect, being an 'old man' in this country still diminishes his power and his status. Aging can also be the time for diminished mental capacity and should it happen to the intellectual narcissist it would be unbearable.

The narcissist then finds it more and more difficult to keep the ego supply coming. Many become angry and bitter; many become depressed and don't even want to live under the circumstances in which they find themselves. Often they are alone reliving their memories, or they keep trying to keep the old days alive. Often they fail and look foolish doing so. They want to do anything but look at themselves, at what is truly inside. Without looking at their psychological core it is difficult to get to their spiritual center.

When you are involved with a narcissist and you are a person who believes in the spiritual or non-physical dimension you will most likely hold on to the idea that your NPD partner just hasn't yet dis-covered his goodness. You may even sense it's pres-ence from time to time, as I did. You may even see it in his eyes, the window to the soul, as I did. And if you've known the person since childhood, you may even remember the time before the narcissism took root, as I did. This will only keep you from let-ting go and moving on. Remember your love can be forever, as mine is, but there is nothing your real love can do to change the person or the situation.

They would much rather have the surface love and affection and attention of someone who sees and believes their false, manufactured self than the love of someone who sees their core and deeper to their soul. That is because what they really want is to have their own pseudo self be the one mirrored back to them. That would be considered success and give them that wonderful sense of safety and security that is proof that their game is working and that their core is safely hidden away and therefore protected.

It is interesting to attempt a conversation with a narcissist on the topic of souls, spirituality or the meaning of life. They may humor you or respond with disdain depending upon what they want from you, but they will never get involved or introspective. I think looking at the bigger picture of possibilities frightens them because it illuminates the smallness of their own lives.

If you're thinking how sad this all is, you are correct. There is very little sadder than a person going through life without ever really knowing their own essence. I can't imagine such a non-introspective, disconnected life. In Nathaniel Branden's book, THE DISOWNED SELF, he writes about the psychological/emotional. disconnect that so many people go through life with.

The only thing I find worse is the disconnect from spirit. To not feel one's connection to their own soul or source is to live a life of no true meaning or purpose or understanding. To the degree that you are psychologically disowned from yourself is the degree to which you will be disconnected psychologically from others and to the degree that you are spiritually disowned is again the degree to which you will experience that disconnect from others at that level.

The narcissist is disconnected and disowned on both these levels. They can therefore, only be connected to others on the physical or intellectual level, depending upon which type they are. So if you are connected to yourself and others and the universe around you, I implore you once again, to not try to save the narcissist who doesn't wish to be saved, but save yourself and disentangle from this person completely, perhaps even with enormous sadness, but not for yourself.

Since the narcissist is not in touch with what we call the soul or the infinite connection he cannot have purpose or meaning to his life in any significant way. Only that which nourishes and enhances the soul can give true meaning to life. The purpose of our lives is about growing the soul, it is about finding our true selves and manifesting it through all we do.

To the narcissist it is all about the ego, whether the ego is expressed through the body or the intellect is irrelevant. A narcissist's life is about things coming in or towards him, a soulful person's life is about what is going out towards the universe as well as coming in. This person is open and expansive, reaching out with love and compassion, while allowing that same goodness to come to them. There are no balance scales and no weighing of how much is coming in versus going out. That is a function of ego alone. I know I've just described the far ends of a continuum. Most of us are neither narcissists nor saints but the closer we get to coming from our source the greater the happiness we feel and the richer our lives become. If you can feel this idea and believe it is something to strive for, rest assured you do not have NPD.

Most narcissists don't even believe in the concept of a soul. If you believe in it, they will say they do if they want you. But they cannot believe it and be a narcissist. They don't believe in any part of us that is eternal, that existed before these bodies came into being and will exist after these bodies turn to dust and that exists now to connect us to the infinite. To them dead is dead and they'd better take it all in now.

I always wanted a soul connection with the man I loved. I envisioned us growing together, feeding our individual souls and each others', being there offering love, support and appreciation to each other, being a source of strength that would lead us to a life of meaning and purpose. Of course, that could not be and in that struggle I gave up my own search while I wallowed in pain, grief and anger.

The end of our relationship put me back on my spiritual path. It was either that or give up and hide under the blanket and that wasn't really an option. I never expected to take this journey alone. I still wish I could turn to him and share all that I've learned and experienced and revel in his growth as well. But some things are just not meant to be. If there is still any pain within me that is the reason. As I've written before, I still want so much for him, maybe more than he wants for himself, definitely different. But we don't get to choose for others no matter how much we care. So I try to wish for him whatever he wishes for himself and walk my own path.

I was on a spiritual path before our reunion almost 11 years ago and I must have sensed that my choice was to continue along that path or walk with him. At that time I believed I could stay at the growth point I had achieved while stepping off that path. This was certainly not well thought out, explicit or even conscious. It could not happen.

I got caught up on the ego path where there was no winning. The definition of a losing battle is having an ego contest with a narcissist.

When you think you love and need another person more than that which is best in yourself, you are on the verge of giving up your soul and traveling a self-destructive path. If you choose to be with a narcissist, remember how difficult it is to give them their ego supply while staying focused on what is best in yourself and your own very real needs. Please don't lose your self or your way as it is a difficult and painful journey back.

The Onset

How and when the narcissistic disorder begins is not fully understood. If there is a biological component it may have to do with oxytocin. Oxytocin is often referred to as the 'bonding hormone'. Women have it in much higher supply than do men. This may be one of the reasons why only 25% of all narcissists are women. Oxytocin is produced in great quantity during childbirth and lactation. It is produced during sexual relations, especially during orgasm, and even while women are interacting with friends. It is a hormone that leads to connections between humans. It allows one person to feel emotionally close to another. Although it is not a gene, it is often referred to as the 'compassion gene'. Narcissists are in short supply of this hormone. In fact this is a similarity experienced by those affected by having a narcissist in their lives. I have heard many times about how the narcissist seems to have been born without the compassion gene. I have said it on numerous occasions to my husband. Once he even acknowledged that he had been told the same thing in the same words previously.

If it is a glitch in the maturation process it could be that the child, who is naturally narcissistic, never develops past that point. If a child normally begins to develop compassion or the ability to see things from the perspective of another and respect those differences, at about age 8, then the narcissist is self-referentially fixed at age 8 or earlier. He will continually see his needs as the center of the universe and see those around him as suppliers of those needs.

It think it is possible that the conditions of onset may be different for the two types of narcissism.

There are professionals who believe narcissism is a learned or adaptive orientation. Some think it is because the child was consistently and constantly idolized and adored. That he was told he was wonderful, the best looking, the smartest, the most capable etc.

Others think he was shamed, traumatized and told he was worthless and insignificant and the narcissism became a defense against seeing himself in this fashion. In this way, he had no choice but to develop a false self both to himself and others. When the major players in his life stop giving him his narcissistic supply, rather than looking inward to see his responsibility and role in the interactions, he finds another person to step into the void. Should he take that look, he will most likely find unwanted feelings and opinions about himself.....so, as said earlier, he just doesn't ever go there.

I think it is more likely than not that somatic narcissism is a result of negativity toward the self rather than truly believing he is wonderful and deserves to be the focus of attention and to receive love from whomever he chooses.

The opinions and feelings of those in the child's life towards him are not necessarily accurately read by the child. They are the interpretations made by the child outside of conscious awareness.

Since young children are always at the center of their universe if there is a family situation where perhaps the child was ignored or neglected, he could have internalized this to mean he was worthless, unimportant and insignificant. He could then be spending the rest of his life trying to undo those

feelings without ever bringing them into awareness and evaluating them from a more mature
perspective.

For the cerebral narcissist, it may begin with those
around him like family members and teachers, telling him of his intellectual superiority without giving notice to his feelings or needs. In this way it is
possible that he identified completely with his mind
and never developed any other component of his
personality or character. He then needed more
and more appreciation of his intellectual abilities.
Since no one saw the other facets of himself he paid
little attention to them as well and found them of
no particular value. His life became about ensuring
that the one thing that was valued in him became
everyones' primary focus and in this way he 'earned'
respect and admiration. But as said earlier, a total
person was never developed and he became more
and more of a strictly intellectual being with no
ability to relate on any other level. Any doubts or
negative feelings he may have had about his other
attributes were quickly repressed and disregarded.
His intellectual self became his only self.

Without going into it, I would like to mention that
there is a form of autism where the person is completely involved in academic studies and has not

formed appropriate social skills. This can be confused with cerebral/intellectual narcissism and may even appear to be similar but the disorder is developmentally different.

The cerebral narcissist doesn't develop a false self in the same manner the somatic narcissist does. For the cerebral, the personality is not as important as his intellectual accomplishments and they are often rather distant and cold. They hide behind the mask of intelligence and very seldom let their guard down in any way that would lead to looking foolish. All they really want is to be respected to the point of being awe-inspiring. They want you to feel inferior and insignificant compared to their greatness. They want no intellectual equality and certainly no competition. They do not attempt to seduce you with a false self and have often been referred to as having 'no personality'.

The somatic, in contrast, is all about a false self and has developed a very effective seductive 'act'. After years of being inauthentic he will believe the false self is real and never wants that idea to be challenged.

It seems to me that in most cases, the idea of sensing any negative opinions or feelings became so overwhelmingly threatening that the narcissist dare not even open that door a crack I can remember having some conversations like this with my ex-husband. Once he even went so far as to say that he feared that if people really knew him they wouldn't like him. When I asked what he thought they wouldn't like, he waited a few beats and then said that it must not be true because he couldn't think of what they would not like about him. It was quickly taken off the table and although I tried a different path, it was never discussed again. I knew that for an instant he told the truth about himself. I thought we might be having a breakthrough and I was so excited by it. Only someone who lives with a narcissist could ever understand what that meant to me. He actually seemed authentic for those very few minutes.

Unfortunately, we had this conversation on the phone. He was in Florida and I was in NJ. I had not wanted to join him in our condo because I was reeling from one thing or another and decided to stay in our home in NJ.

After that conversation I thought that maybe our relationship could have a chance after all. I saw some light shining in and said I would come to Florida if we could continue this discussion in person. He agreed and I flew down. I had decided that I would not bring the subject up and would wait for him to do it. I was hopeful but still angry and upset about what had happened to lead me to stay in NJ. After two or three days in Florida which were pleasant but not close, he had still not brought up that which was the reason for my trip down. But, he wanted to be sexually intimate and that was not where my focus was. I turned him down, which in retrospect was the wrong thing to do. I know a lot more now than I did back then and realize that to him that might have brought about the sense of closeness that he needed in order to trust me enough to begin another conversation. Things went downhill from there.

That was a little personal aside but I think it shows that the narcissist holds some very negative feelings and a great deal of fear of looking at them.

Even if, by some miracle, they see this, it doesn't alter the fact that they still don't have much, if any, true compassion or can begin to see another person as really important in their own right regardless of what they can bring to him. If it is strictly a maturation malfunction I don't know if that window of opportunity is still open or if a natural developmental process is aborted will it be forever too late.

These are areas that the myriad of professionals look at and that everyone touched by a narcissist asks in the hope that there are answers out there for them.

I have asked for stories from people who have seen changes in narcissists over time and through some form of therapy. I have not gotten any. I have gotten many of the opposite nature. There are those who leave them and those who are left and those who struggle to stay with them, but no one I know has heard of anyone who has seen one grow and evolve. I was hoping to be the first.

How can you not remember?

It's strange how this chapter came to be written. It is day three of our living under the same roof and an interesting interaction occurred between us that reminded me of many others through the years.

He had decided to divorce in May 2009 but we continued to live together until the end of October when he left for what used to be our Florida condo and was now his home. Our divorce was final in the beginning of October. Due to circumstances I was going to visit friends in Florida at the end of December, 2010 and since he was in DC visiting family we drove down together.

During that next week I spent one of the most significantly devastating times of my life. I was in overwhelming emotional pain which he knew and saw for himself. At that time I told him that once our New Jersey house sold, I never wanted to see him or speak to him again for the rest of my life and he was not to contact me at all except for the house closing. If he had to communicate with me about the house it was to be by e-mail and I would answer in kind. At that point I realized all contact with him had to be stopped completely. I knew we still owned the house together and that we would have to deal with that to some extent. I didn't realize at that time that he would want to avail himself of the house and actually spend time in it, which was his legal right.

Yesterday, he mentioned not having seen me since he left in October. I said he saw me in January. He was surprised and said it was October and he didn't remember seeing me in January. I insisted and after a few minutes of thinking about it he said he had forgotten all about that week. For about 5 or 10 seconds I actually felt hurt and then I began to laugh to myself.

Many events began to come back to me where he had 'forgotten' something that was said or done either by himself or one of his children that was hurtful or insulting to me. I started to think about the dynamics of these very important lapses in memory and it became clear very soon how and why they happened.

In the past I could never understand how he could forget such important events and would bring them up for review. (often) He would then usually admit that they did happen but he had 'put them out of his mind' because he didn't want to think about them. Well, of course he didn't. If he did it would show him in a way he didn't want to appear to himself. If he admitted that what was said and/or done was cruel and thoughtless he would have to ask himself why he would do or say them. Of course he could not do that because narcissists never look at themselves in an introspective way. So they just forget it ever happened.

In the case of forgetting his children's words or behavior, remember narcissists never blame their children for any wrongdoing and so they have to forget those also. They do this very well. If you remember the events, as it is likely you will, you will think there is something wrong with their memory and question how they could possibly have 'forgotten' what occurred. It will be like spitting in the wind and will just frustrate and anger you. They absolutely cannot allow themselves to take the responsibility for their words and actions and if they cannot blame you in a way that they can justify, they will just not remember it.

Also, just because something was important to you don't believe for a minute that it was important to the narcissist. Even if, like the event that happened to me in Florida, it was traumatic for you, if it didn't impact on him in receiving his supply, it never made a dent in his consciousness. If it wasn't directly about him it might as well not have even happened.

So after just three days I received enough information for another chapter that I hope will be of benefit to you.

And how in the world can I still love you?

This chapter is being written right after the last one. It is not 'out of order' as most of the chapters are.

It is 1 AM and I am wondering about my feelings for my own very special narcissist.

Maybe it's my understanding of the disorder, maybe it's knowing who he was as a young boy, maybe it's because I feel like I know his soul even if he doesn't, maybe I'm just sticking with my fantasy regardless of knowing the reality of who he is today and maybe it just doesn't matter, but I am feeling a deep and abiding love for someone whose values in this physical reality, I can't imagine being rewarding in any meaningful way. But I recognize that people get value from their lives in different ways and make their own choices.

I am a very smart woman, especially in this area, but I still feel like an addict and I can feel the yearning in my body. I can feel the love in my heart. I can feel the connection in my soul.

I know how normal and natural it feels to have him in the house. To watch him walk by, the hear the shower running, for him to ask if I would like a glass of wine or some frozen yogurt, to see some of his personal belongings that haven't been part of my home for almost 10 months. It feels right to me. That is really too bad.

We are getting along cordially, even friendly, perhaps even warmly, it is good and not good. He wants to be my friend. He can be for the next two weeks and then no more. Being his friend will not work for me. It will not keep me on my path to growth.

This may be some of the most challenging days of my life. Hopefully I will continue to understand the narcissistic personality and maybe even begin to understand how people like you and me can continue to care for them.

I have realized that how I feel is meaningless in light of how I choose to behave and the thoughts I choose to think. To fight how I feel about him is nonsensical and futile. It just exists. Hopefully someday it won't but I'm not a betting person and would never take odds in favor of it disappearing. It is what it is.

But I take heart in knowing that I am so much stronger, so much happier, so much more at peace than I was when we were together and I will never fall apart because of lies and deceits, or secrets and insults and especially betrayals ever again. That alone is empowering.

I'm sure the days to follow will bring even more insights and understandings and I will pass them on to you.

It is now almost a month since I wrote the last piece. He advised me that he will be gone for three weeks and then back here for another two. The challenge increases....This is beginning to feel like I am writing into my journal but I think it is important that the reader be a part of this.

Love or Need?

When I realized that it was most important to me that he be happy, I realized a couple of other things simultaneously. The first one was that regardless of how much I wished for his happiness I had no control over it. I knew what I preferred but I also knew that I couldn't have my happiness be contingent upon his. My happiness was my own business and not something anyone else had input into. I had always known this, taught it, talked about it, wrote about it but I knew it in concept and in words only. I didn't really experience the truth of that on a cellular level. Could it have been that all those people who were important to me were actually controlling my life through my 'need' for them to be happy? I wanted the best for them because I loved them but did I need it for my own well-being? Did they then have an obligation to me to live in such a way that would give me what I needed? If that were true, who was I really loving? Sounded a lot like it was myself. How free was I really if I needed the people I loved to live happily to make me happy? How free were they?

So my second realization was that the people I loved were free to live however they chose and it was none of my business. If they were unhappy or even depressed I had to let them live their own experiences without 'demanding' they be happy to fulfill my need for them to be a certain way. It was their right to be unhappy if they chose to. I would always be there if they wanted to learn to choose happiness and I would always be there if they didn't.

Writing a book about narcissism gave me my third revelation. No one is in my life to provide me with what I need. Because I have chosen to be happy I work on doing, being and having what fulfills that for me. But this does not extend to other people. They have their own needs and wants to fulfill. If we find ourselves on the same path we can travel together and enjoy the journey.

In my relationship with my husband I talked the talk but didn't walk the walk. I had a choice to make back then. I could have opted to have a life with a narcissist I loved and accept what was available to me and not ask him for the emotional intimacy and commitment I wanted so badly from him or I could have left lovingly, accepting that I could not be satisfied with the limited type of relationship he could offer. In my own neediness I forgot how much I loved him. I could not, at that time, allow him to be who he had no choice but to be. When I withdrew my supply, he eventually left. I knew he would. It took months for me to regain my perspective and reclaim myself.

I am telling you this so you can understand that you also have a choice. If you are still involved with your narcissist you will be in a much better emotional place if you consciously decide which route you want to take. If you decide to stay, realize he will never change and you will have to accept with all your heart that what he can give you is limited. You will have to decide whether that is enough or not enough for you. Only you can do that. No one else has the answer.

If you decide to leave, know that you are leaving because you realize that you want more from a relationship than he can give you. He is damaged in that department and even if he wants you to stay and promises to change, he is unable to. If you stay expecting him to change you will eventually wear both of you out and become angry and hurt. So leave with love and honor. And then, as I've mentioned before, leave totally and completely.

So what are you feeling? Is it love going outward while also going inward towards yourself or is it the fulfillment of a need that you want to come to you from someone else? Whose job is it to make you happy? Whose job is it to fulfill your needs?

You may one day be lucky enough to meet someone who can love you and give you what you want but it won't be a narcissist unless what you want is a low or moderate level of relationship for yourself while his focus will be on the fulfillment of his needs by you.

Relationships to the narcissist are not about love, they are about need. His. It is a one way street. If you love him so much that you want to spend your life giving to him hoping it will be enough and you will finally stop hearing about what you are not giving him; if you love him so much that you will not suffer anxiety that he will find someone to give him more than you are; if you love him so much that you will continue to enjoy giving when you are not receiving.....then you will be happy with him. Otherwise, please understand that you will remain unfulfilled and probably angry. If you want more from a relationship than that, forgive him and move on.

Remember, leaving is like the withdrawal of a drug alongside the trauma of separation, but you will recover especially if you leave with understanding and self-respect and without blame and recriminations.

Jan

Jan called me five months ago when her relationship came to an abrupt end. I scheduled an appointment with her and asked that in the meantime she send me a brief outline of what she wanted to work on. She sent a three page e-mail that sounded somewhat familiar to me. Although I didn't want to form an opinion yet, it was difficult for me not to see the word NARCISSIST screaming to me from the pages. I had worked with enough partners and children of them to recognize the NPD in her boyfriend and I was only eight months past hearing and seeing the same things from my husband.

I told Jan that I would either be the best or the worst therapist she could possibly have. I then did something very unprofessional and told her I was dealing with the same issue in my own life although I was eight months into it and that although I believed I could understand her better than anyone else that I may also be biased. She said she really wanted to work with me as I came highly recommend to her. I told her I would be as objective as possible and we could give it a try.

She had been living with her boyfriend, Mitch, for about six years. They owned a home together although he paid for most of it. She was very much in love with him and had believed he felt the same way. He had been married before and had three children. She had been married for a short time and did not have children of her own. Jan wanted to marry, Mitch did not. He did not have a good working relationship with his ex-wife and did not want the marriage experience again.

Jan spent a great deal of time with his children when it was his weekend to have them. He would always find other things to do and Jan said she felt like the baby-sitter. Although she did enjoy them, she was beginning to feel used and unappreciated.

After her first appointment I asked her if she knew anything about NPD. She said she didn't but that she would research it. At her next appointment she declared that Mitch had almost every trait listed and what she had read described him to a T. She even told me that she was sure he was a somatic narcissist. She felt both better and worse knowing this. I also was sure that if we were both correct about him, that the relationship was better off over.

She admitted to feeling some relief in knowing that she was not to blame for the problems in the relationship and with her declining level of trust in him. However, she was experiencing many of the physical manifestations that I mentioned earlier. She had terrible stomach pain and nausea, a palpable feeling of lonliness and sadness and regret for giving up six years of her life to a relationship that went nowhere.

One of her biggest issues was that she had read, and I agreed with, the idea of total closure and no contact. Mitch wanted to be her friend. He texted her many times a day and phoned often. However, his friendship did not include buying her out of the house or offering to sell it so she could recover her investment. It did include helping her find another place to live. Even knowing that she would be better off avoiding him at all costs, she could not close the door on being his 'friend'. She also continued to see his children and spend a great deal of time with them. She became friendly with his ex-wife while making plans to see the children and they would discuss Mitch often.

It appeared to me as if she could not let go. Even when she inevitably discovered that he was already in another relationship and had been for a while and that he was taking the new girlfriend on a vacation that was planned for them, she still could not move on.

I knew exactly how she felt as my experience was eerily similar. She said she knew she should not be communicating with him and seeing his children and his ex-wife but she still believed he was 'mixed-up' and would soon come to his senses.

The last time I saw her, I had completed about 25 pages of this book and let her read it. She told me it upset her because she realized that everything I had written was true and certainly pertained to Mitch and to her.

She stopped all communication with me at that time. I hope she has finally moved on. I think she believed I was judging her weakness in not being able to leave him completely although he was with someone else and only wanted to remain her friend. I believe she was judging herself and projecting it to me. I probably made a mistake in letting her know that being eight months ahead of her, I knew she could eventually take her life back as I was doing. Maybe she thought she couldn't. I really don't know because I have lost contact with her.

I hope she's doing well, but I remember her saying to me that she lost her soul to him and would never recover. I have heard that said more times than I care to count. I have even said it myself but it wasn't the truth. Although I am still connected to him in a deeply spiritual way, I did recover. It does, however, take an enormous commitment to life and happiness and the truth that you know will come in time if you take those necessary steps toward healing.

Recovery

The road to recovery is paved with good-feeling thoughts.

Your relationship with your narcissist has ended because it was a bad relationship where neither of you was getting what you wanted and needed, not because you were both happy and fulfilled. I understand that if you were the one to end it and you were still in love, you did it painfully and with many second thoughts. If your partner ended it you felt hurt, betrayed and lost. Please know that this was taking its toll on both of you in both emotional and physical ways and could not continue indefinitely without severe negative consequences to your spirit and your body.

So now your time has come to make that choice I wrote about earlier. Will you give up your power in despair and depression or will you pull yourself up and commit to your own happiness and well-being? Making the choice, even without taking any action, is your first step. I have never seen anyone make a conscious, volitional choice to be sad and anxious. Those choices are made by default. They are made by not saying a resounding YES to good feelings. It takes energy to refuse to lay down and give up but I assure you it is energy well spent.

In the midst of your pain it is difficult to find any energy or resolve at all and almost impossible to imagine being the powerful up-lifted person you know you once were. You think there is no way to get there from where you presently are.

So just start with the choice to eventually get there. Just making that choice will change the direction in which you are facing. If you aren't able to do it then make the choice to make the choice by telling yourself that you want to be able to choose well being tomorrow. Then do it for all the tomorrows until you are able to complete the very basic choice to orient yourself towards being happy.

It will take as long as it takes. For one person it may become transformational. The desire to experience well being and the belief that it is possible is so strong that the person becomes uplifted immediately and knows without a doubt that she is on the way. The pain is still there; the loneliness is still there; perhaps the anger is also still there, but along with that is the absolute certainty that good feelings are just waiting to be caught up with and experienced.

For others it is a long and difficult process but it will happen. All that is necessary is to continue to make the choice to want to make the choice to be powerful and joyful as soon as you are able. Each day will bring you closer.

One day you will know you are ready and you will be strong enough to say 'I choose to live a happy life'. When you really believe you are ready to choose, and in fact do choose it, you will feel a shift inside you because your direction has just changed.

If you want to drive from New York to Boston you cannot face south. Just heading north for as long as it takes will bring you closer to your destination and the farther you drive the stronger the pull to arrive will be.

From the point of change you will sense the beginnings of a lighter and brighter self. A sense of relief will be noticed and you will find yourself believing that you are indeed on the path to happiness.

Then notice how and what you are thinking and the effect those thoughts have on your emotions. You will learn quickly what thoughts bring you back to despair and powerlessness and which ones move you forward and lighten your state of being. Keep choosing the thoughts that make you feel better and notice what happens over time.

Remember that the choice to think or not, and then the choice of what to think, is the first step toward personal freedom.

I believe one of the things that will become evident is that thoughts of blame will set you back. It doesn't matter if you are blaming yourself or your former partner. It is true, as I've written earlier, that narcissists don't take responsibility for the outcomes of their behavior and continually blame you for everything that went wrong. They truly believe that if you had given them what they wanted they would have been happy and stayed with you. That is most likely true, but also impossible. They can blame you because they come from an immature perspective. Remember, they probably haven't emotionally developed past adolescence at best and age 8 at worst. You, on the other hand, now understand that to blame them is useless. They really could not help being who and how they are. It is, remember, a disorder. No matter what they put you through, you are the healthier person and keeping that in the forefront of your mind is one of the thoughts that will help you move forward.

To blame yourself is equally useless. Maybe you could have seen the signs of NPD earlier, maybe you could have evaluated them more effectively, maybe you could have been more loving, patient, understanding, giving, and allowing and less demanding, angry, insecure, suspicious and hurt. Maybe you could have been superhuman. But you were just being normal; wanting things that anyone would want in an intimate relationship.

The biggest mistake partners of narcissists make, and I have certainly made it also, is to fall in love with someone and then assign them qualities they do not have and continue to be disappointed when those qualities are not exhibited. Even when we finally realize that these qualities just don't exist within that person, we keep trying to elicit them and then get angry when we are disappointed yet again and our Prince Charming doesn't behave in a way that is impossible for him.

We cannot choose a person (any person, not just a narcissist) and insist that that particular person be who we want them to be. They have to be who they are and if we don't like it and can't accept it, our only alternative is to leave and continue to look for the person who has the qualities we are looking for. Again, it is not possible to harangue a person without certain assets into having them. But please don't blame yourself for trying. Just learn from your experience and move on.

Telling yourself blaming thoughts whether about yourself or your former partner will not bring you good feelings. You can control what you are thinking to a greater degree than you believe and therefore control how you are feeling. Just notice how you are feeling, especially if it is negative, and trace your thoughts back to the one that caused your bad feeling. Then change it to whatever degree you are able to at any given moment. There will be times you can make a big jump in your thinking and times you can make a tiny hop and times when those nasty, negative thoughts keep popping back into your mind. At those times, if you can't think any positive thought, go and do something that will take all your concentration and stop thinking about the issue altogether. Then somewhat later, go back to attempting to think something on the subject that will lead to a more positive feeling.

This is exercise for the mind. It is a training session. You wouldn't expect yourself to go from lifting 5 lbs of weight in the gym to lifting 50 lbs overnight. You wouldn't expect to put on a pair of skis and become an Olympian. Training yourself to think thoughts that will lead to feelings of well being also takes practice. You will know you are succeeding when you begin to feel better.

Also, try not to discuss your previous relationship over and over again. Rehashing what has happened in the past will certainly not move you forward into healing. If you must discuss it with someone, try to concentrate on what you have learned from it and how you have grown. Begin by purchasing a notebook, call it your Positivity Notebook (see the next chapter) and write all the lessons you have learned. Picture yourself happy and whole. Your imagination can be a good friend to your progress.

As you begin to focus less and less on what happened and what was done to you and how sad and lonely you are, those feelings will begin to fade into the past. Remind yourself that you have a choice to recover and live a happy life or to stay where you are.

Here's one more point to consider. Since we often realize that our former narcissistic partner actually wants us to be happy because it exonerates his bad behavior and makes him feel better (it has nothing to do with you or your true happiness), we refuse to be happy to give him that satisfaction. There is a false premise that if we remain miserable and blaming that he will feel badly about what he has done. It is, we believe, the only power left to us to not give him yet another thing that he wants. You are not a sacrificial lamb. Ultimately the only one who really cares about whether you are happy and experiencing well being is you. He is off living his life, happily I might add, and really not thinking about you at all. Please choose happiness for yourself and don't concern yourself that you are giving him something else that will add to his life in some way. His life no longer matters to you. Yours really doesn't matter to him. Your being miserable is only hurting you and you don't deserve to suffer any more especially by your own hand.

Positivity Notebook Exercises

The following exercises are not original. I must thank Abraham/Hicks for them. They are brilliant and work magic.

In this book you will be writing about positive aspects, appreciation and thankfulness.

One of the ways to bring positive, good feeling thoughts into your life is by creating a notebook in which you write about these three categories.

Positive Aspects:

Pick a topic in your life. It could be a situation, a person, a thing or an experience.

It could even be a topic you are unhappy about.

In your newly purchased notebook write on top of the page:

The Positive Aspects of_____

Then list them. Attempt to find even the tiniest positiveness you can find as well as the more obvious. You can use as many topics at a time as you like, as long as you do at least one every morning.

The first time I asked a client to do this, she wanted to know when she got to write the negative aspects. I said 'never'. At first this did not make her happy as she was eager to write all of them in the most minute detail. I had explained to her that the purpose of the exercise was to have her focus on positiveness but her orientation at that time was to completely look at everything negative in her life. It took about a month for the feedback from her to turn around along with the focus of her day to day life. It is wonderful to watch people change direction from being comfortable looking at what they don't like to being ecstatic looking at what they do like.

Appreciation:

Your next list will be of whatever you appreciate in your day. It can be as small as a nice gesture by a salesperson or as significant as a person you love. Take time during your day to notice anything you can appreciate and add it to your notebook. You may wish to carry a small pad with you to jot things down as you notice them and then transfer them to your notebook.

If you see something you like, something that brings a smile or a chuckle to you, don't forget to write it down.

Once again, you will not be writing down anything negative. If you should see something you don't like in the course of your day try to ignore it or at least don't focus on it. Stay facing the direction at which you ultimately wish to arrive.

Thankfulness:

At night before going to sleep, write down what you were thankful or grateful for in your day.

In this way you have begun your day with a positive thought, you have experienced feelings of appreciation throughout your day and you have ended your day with thankfulness.

You may have a great deal of 'overlap' in your lists. That is fine. It is better than fine because you are focusing more intensely on what you like.

Don't forget to read your lists back as often as you can.

Do this every day and you will see how quickly life begins to feel better to you.

If you enjoy the exercise, pass it along to others and compare notes. The more positive, appreciation seeking, thankful people you have in your life, the quicker you will feel your heart soaring once again and you will enjoy being a source of positiveness to those you love and care for.

Believe that your pain will fade further away and be replaced with wonderful up-lifting feelings because that will surely happen.

You may also add another section to your notebook when you are feeling somewhat better and emotionally stronger and more stable. That would be the section describing exactly what and who you want to have in your life. The more details you use, the better. Now that you know exactly what you don't want, it will become easier for you to know what it is that you do want. Think about it, imagine it, daydream about it, talk about it, write about it. Believe that it will come to you.

Even if you don't yet have what you want, try not to think thoughts that lead you to ponder that lack. Those will not lead you to feelings of well being.

Your mind doesn't realize the difference between what is real and what is imagined. If you concentrate on good things good feelings will find you and the reverse is also true. Try this for a month and see how you feel.

There is an old adage that the better you feel, the better you feel; and the worse you feel, the worse you feel. It really is your choice.

In Summary
(and then some)

After much research, interviews, introspection and writing, I realized that although you and I felt as if there was a huge, thick, invisible wall between our values and those of the person we loved, he or she didn't understand us either. He couldn't get why we were so unhappy and angry or why the words trust and intimacy showed up so often in our vocabulary.

The narcissists behavior is a compensation for the realization that he is unable to give you what you want and need. The lies and deceptions are because he can't show you who he really is or what he really does. The charm is because he cannot be authentic. The intellectual overbearing is because he cannot connect to his own feelings. The need for 'false freedom' is because he hasn't the capacity to commit and doesn't feel internally free. His hiding from you is because he is hiding from himself. Being psychologically visible to another can open the door to being this visible to himself and that is too frightening.

To a narcissist, intimacy is not a value, an open and honest relationship is not something he wants and commitment is threatening. A narcissist is compulsively led to this false sense of freedom. A narcissist doesn't value being seen and truly loved. A narcissist feels safe being alone in every way but the physical. A narcissist doesn't want the emotional or spiritual connection that you do.

To those of use who are not narcissists these seem like strange choices but they were not made deliberately until he was asked to behave in ways that are natural in relationships and found himself unable. The original decision was actually made by default because of fear.

Please don't look at this as a rejection of you, just try to make peace with the fact that there are times you can't have what you want if it regards another person. They are free to live whatever kind of life appeals to them and so are you.

Your choices must be made with deliberate intent for your own happiness and well- being. If you still have the choice of being with your narcissist think carefully and honestly about what you can and cannot handle and then make the choice with caution.

One last area I would like to touch upon is about the capacity to love and accept. I remember when I was a young teenager and met the boy I fell in love with. At that time I believe I loved him to whatever capacity I had at that time and age. When we reunited many years later and I was traveling a spiritual and psychological growth path, my capacity to love was greater and my love for him was richer and deeper. When things went very wrong in our relationship and I stepped off my path, my capacity diminished to almost nothing I could feel or act on. Since I have taken a quantum leap in my own growth my capacity and my love is greater than it has even been.

You will find that as you recover and grow, the same thing will happen to you. When you are no longer angry and hurt and you understand your relationship with your own narcissist with more clarity, you will find that your experience will allow you the ability to love in a much greater way.

It will be up to you to decide what you can accept and allow in your personal space. Once you are absolutely clear on where you stand and accept totally that you will not attempt to change him you can then make a decision about the relationship for yourself. He may not agree. He knows what he is willing to give you. But remember he is probably an easy and accomplished liar. If you stay with him, even without looking for the lie, you will eventually run into it. If you are walking a spiritual path I will bet that at some point your intuition or an 'accidental' discovery will lead you right where you need to be to learn what you need to learn. If this happens, please don't be angry. He is being who he is and can't be who he isn't. At that time you can re-evaluate your level of acceptance and and make a new decision. You can always choose to only look at what you like and not give notice to what you don't like.....as long as it is a conscious and volitional choice. But you should be paying a lot of attention to how you are really feeling. If you are feeling hurt again, ask yourself if you are once again being the major contributing factor to your own loss of well-being. It is not as complicated as it sounds.

Once you are at the point of allowing him to be who he is and you have set your own parameters of acceptance you cannot be hurt again. If his behavior is outside your limits, you walk away.....and once more do it completely. Don't fool yourself that you are where you are not or you will once more feel deceived and betrayed when your hopes are dashed. Unless you know explicitly and exactly what you will accept and understand the narcissists orientation to those, it is important that you don't subject yourself to it again. Don't even attempt this type of reconciliation until you have gone through the recovery process and you are sure you are healed and strong. Otherwise it is important for you to stay away and release both of you from the dysfunction where you will be the one suffering once again.

I hope this book has helped you as much as it has helped me to write it. I will write the final chapter after my time of co-habitation is over.

I wish you all the very best.

Epilogue-
The Final Chapter
(at least for now)

How many times in one lifetime can I fall in love with the same person?

I am once again alone in my home (or as he likes to say 'our home').

He is the same man he has always been. He still owns my heart and most likely always will.

I know he loves me as much as he is able to love anyone.

I know exactly what I want and I know what I don't want.

I don't want to be married to him; I don't want to live with him; I want a part-time monogamous relationship with him. Are you laughing? I am.

However, I feel wonderful. I feel happy. I know I am solely responsible for my own well-being. I know I have recovered.

I know you can also.

PS: The original name for this book was going to be Irreparable Wounds. They are decidedly not.